# RIBA
# HEALTH
# AND
# SAFETY
# GUIDE

© RIBA Publishing, 2020

Published by RIBA Publishing, 66 Portland Place, London, W1B 1AD

ISBN 978 1 85946 921 7

British Library Cataloguing-in-Publication Data

A catalogue record for this book is available from the British Library.

Commissioning Editor: Alex White
Assistant Editor: Clare Holloway
Production: Richard Blackburn
Designed by Kneath Associates
Typeset by Fakenham Prepress Solutions, Norfolk
Printed and bound by W&G Bird, Antrim
All illustrations, including cover, by Natalie Gall

*While every effort has been made to check the accuracy and quality
of the information given in this publication, neither the Author nor the
Publisher accept any responsibility for the subsequent use or misuse
of this information, for any errors or omissions that it may contain,
or for any misunderstandings arising from it. Independent specialist
advice should be sought in relation to any specific information
provided in this publication.*

**www.ribapublishing.com**

# RIBA
# HEALTH
# AND
# SAFETY
# GUIDE

RIBA Publishing

# CONTENTS

# DEDICATION

This book is dedicated to everyone whose health and well-being may have been affected by collective failings in the construction industry to protect the safety of those we rely on to construct, maintain, refurbish and/or demolish our built environment.

# ACKNOWLEDGEMENTS

I would like to acknowledge the help and contributions of Rahim Rahemtulla and Alex Tait at the RIBA, my many colleagues at EPR Architects, in particular Emily Armer and Richard Irving, members of the RIBA Regulations and Standards Group, in particular Andy Jobling, Gavin Bull at the Health and Safety Executive and Alex White at RIBA Publishing, and thank them all for their invaluable insight, support and assistance in preparing this companion guide.

I would also like to thank my husband, Neil, for his unwavering support and encouragement, which gives me the confidence to lend my voice to all of those working tirelessly to improve our profession, the construction industry and the built environment.

Dieter Bentley-Gockmann
EPR Architects
June 2020

# INTRODUCTION

As architects, we enjoy the privilege of being able to help shape the world around us. We have the opportunity to build communities and positively impact on the daily lives of all those that interact with our work through collaboration with our clients and their design and construction teams. As designers, lead designers and principal designers, we have an opportunity to influence the decision-making processes of our clients and their design and construction teams.

With these opportunities comes a responsibility to see that any decisions over which we exert control or influence are made bearing in mind the best interests of everyone that will be affected by our projects. In particular, we have a responsibility to ensure that every person that comes into contact with our projects, from inception through to occupation, maintenance, adaptation, conversion or subsequent demolition, is able to do so safely and with no detrimental effect on their health and well-being. This includes a duty to keep ourselves and our colleagues safe.

The responsibility to always be mindful of safety issues and create architecture that safeguards the well-being of the public goes to the core of everything that we do as architects; be that as a student, academic, researcher, practitioner, architectural assistant, project runner, practice principal, sole practitioner, employed or self-employed architect.

None of us set out to put ourselves at risk, design an unsafe project or knowingly cause harm. We must be conscious, however, that in our often highly pressured industry, with increasingly complex design, procurement and project delivery processes, we risk being distracted from paying sufficient attention to the elements of our professional services that ensure our projects are – and remain – safe.

The forthcoming RIBA health and safety test for architects is for everyone working and studying across the profession, and this companion guide has been produced by architects for architects to be a study aid for architectural students and an aide memoire for qualified architects preparing for the forthcoming test. Perhaps, more importantly, this guide is intended to remind us all that safe practice and design should be at the heart of what we do. We all have a duty to act professionally at all times and we all have a responsibility to ensure that everyone affected by the built environments we create is safe and feels safe.

Chapter 1 considers how you should prepare for every site visit you intend to undertake, whether to an unoccupied or occupied site, to ensure you are adequately equipped to undertake your visit safely. Chapter 2 details how you should conduct your site visit, whether to an unoccupied or occupied site, to ensure you are able to undertake your visit safely. The more significant or typical hazards you might face during a site visit are covered in Chapter 3 and provide guidance on how you might consider managing these to ensure you remain safe. In Chapter 4, we explore the principles of design risk management, the general principles of prevention and the role of effective communication and coordination. Chapter 5 looks at the minimum standards with which you need to be familiar, including statute and the regulatory environment, non-statutory guidance and codes of conduct. Chapter 6 consider the legal duties imposed on designers and principal designers under the CDM Regulations. Finally Chapter 7 covers the principles of fire science, the fire performance of construction materials and aspects of fire safety design.

# CHAPTER 1:
# PREPARING
# TO VISIT SITE

Undertaking site visits is vital to our role as architects and fulfils several functions, from enabling us to understand and analyse the context within which our projects will reside through to inspecting the progress of work on site to ascertain that a construction project is proceeding in accordance with our designs and in meeting our clients' requirements.

Our interaction with the environment and the unexpected circumstances it might present is one of the most challenging, exciting and enjoyable aspects of being an architect. However, it is also when we are most likely to face potentially hazardous situations that pose a risk to our safety, health and well-being.

When we talk about visiting site, we tend to envisage visiting managed demolition and/or construction sites. Whilst these pose particular risks, arguably it is vacant sites you will visit before construction has commenced – or possibly even before a project has been conceived – which are not under active daily management, that present greater risks.

For the purpose of this guide we refer to **occupied sites** – those that are occupied by the owner or tenants and are actively managed, including construction sites; and **unoccupied sites** – those that are vacant or disused and not actively managed. In either case the person responsible for control of the site or their representative may or may not be present during your site visit.

Naturally, returning safely from any site visit is always our intention. Ensuring this happens requires common sense, responsible site behaviour and being ready to respond to hazards if and when they arise.

In this chapter, we consider six aspects of how to prepare for every site visit you intend to undertake – whether to an unoccupied or occupied site – to ensure you are adequately equipped to undertake your visit safely:

Do not proceed with a visit to an unoccupied site unless you can ascertain that it is safe to do so

## 1.1 Site surveys and research

Gathering site information before your visit, based on formal surveys or previous experience (your own, that of your colleagues or of the site owner), is invaluable. Familiarise yourself with all available information regarding the site before your visit.

Request copies of all site information in the possession of the site owner. This may include site plans, site photographs, footage from digital drone surveys, condition survey reports and details regarding the presence and nature of any known or suspected site contamination, in particular any asbestos-containing materials (ACMs).

Consult any historic maps, satellite images and/or survey information to identify ancient structures and landscape features that may be present on site, bearing in mind once you are on site that such structures and features may be unstable due to decomposition, weathering or vandalism.

If you are aware of existing buildings or structures on the site that you are due to visit, obtain as much up-to-date survey information regarding their condition prior to your visit as is practicable. Identify any confined spaces or unsafe structures that you will need to avoid. This is especially important for vacant, disused, derelict or semi-derelict structures where there may be the risk of fragile floors, stairs or roofs, or where demolition has already taken place and there may be risk from partially concealed basements, the presence of asbestos or live unknown services. If you need to inspect or gather information from these areas, consider how you may do this without putting your safety at risk, for example, by utilising drones and digital technology.

5m

10m

Consult all available site information prior to your visit and verify its accuracy once you are on site

If you are visiting a building that was constructed or refurbished before 2000, request a copy of the site owner's asbestos management survey to establish whether there is any risk of exposure to asbestos during your visit. The site owner has a legal duty to determine if an asbestos survey is needed.[1] If asbestos is present on site, the survey will record what it is, where it is, how much there is and the condition it is in. If asbestos has been identified on site, make sure you are familiar with its location and condition. Check the survey for details of any caveats or limitations regarding its use, including any areas of the site that may not have been surveyed. Never visit a site where there is a risk of exposure to airborne fibres that are released when asbestos is damaged or disturbed.

All employers have a duty to provide adequate asbestos awareness training to anybody visiting site. Ensure that you undertake this training before your site visit so that you understand how to avoid the risk of exposure to asbestos. Risks associated with exposure to asbestos are covered in more detail in Chapter 3.

Verify the accuracy and currency of all site information you receive from others and bear in mind that conditions may have changed since the site was last visited or surveyed. Consider the age of any record information – in particular any as-built plans – and reflect on whether there may have been subsequent alterations on site since the records were produced.

If you have any concerns regarding the quality or accuracy of site information at your disposal, speak to the site owner or person in control of the site and identify what further information you require for consideration prior to your visit.

Establish whether there are any live services or mechanical plant that may pose a risk on site or whether such services/plant have been safely decommissioned and/or disconnected.

Once you are aware of and understand the potential hazards that may be present on site, prepare an action plan to determine how you will respond to hazards, should they arise. Make sure this is agreed and understood by any colleagues who intend to accompany you on your visit. Your

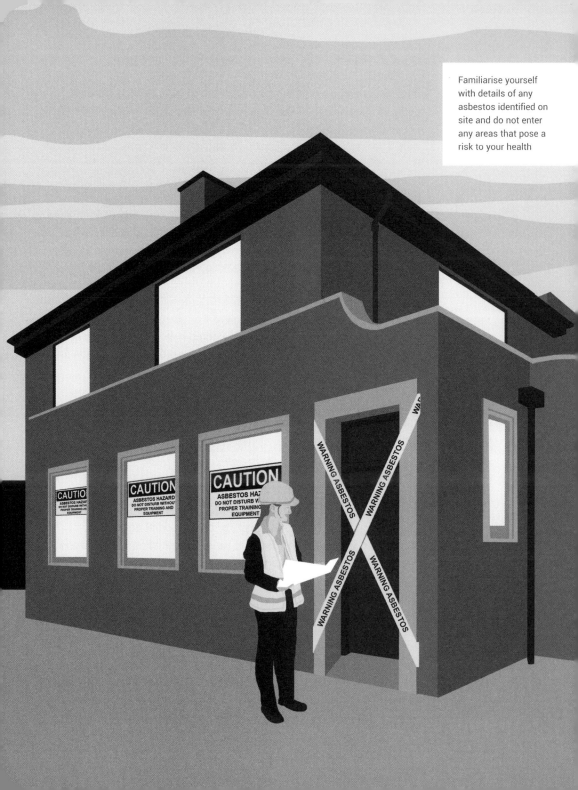

Familiarise yourself with details of any asbestos identified on site and do not enter any areas that pose a risk to your health

Do not approach or attempt to use any services or mechnical plant that is in poor repair

DANGER OF DEATH

Isolate supply before opening door

action plan should be site-specific, recorded in writing, reviewed and, if appropriate, updated prior to every site visit. Provide copies of the action plan to others who you know will be visiting the site, for example, survey companies that you may have instructed on behalf of your client.

Ensure that you are aware of any regulatory restrictions or duties that the site owner or you, as a site visitor, need to be knowledgeable about. This includes any legal duties you may have as an employer with respect to safe-guarding the welfare of your employees (explored in more detail in Chapters 3 and 4).

## 1.2 Planning work

Before you go to site, determine and appropriately plan the purpose of your visit. Ensure you have adequate time to undertake the tasks you propose to embark on without rushing, bearing in mind how site conditions may compromise how efficiently you may be able to work. This is particularly important during the winter when inclement weather or limited daylight hours are more likely to restrict how long you can work safely on site. Avoid the temptation to continue your visit beyond the time it is safe to do so in an effort to get your planned task completed if it takes you longer than anticipated.

Pre-plan the activities you intend to undertake to ensure you have access to any survey equipment that you require once you are on site. This might include arranging for appropriate temporary working platforms, lighting and/or power to be installed before you arrive.

If you require any destructive opening-up to be undertaken on site to complete any intrusive survey work, wherever possible arrange for the opening-up works to be carried out prior to your visit. If the site owner's asbestos management survey has identified the presence of asbestos on site, ensure that a refurbishment/demolition survey is completed prior to any destructive opening-up work. If asbestos is identified, confirm with the site owner that it has been removed by a licenced contractor and that the area you are visiting has been certified fit for reoccupation prior to your visit.

Pre-plan your activities to ensure appropriate access is available for your visit

Ensure a qualified operative is available to assist you with any specialist access equipment required during your visit

If you require access to be provided via mobile plant, such as a mobile elevating work platform (MEWP), ensure that you are accompanied by an operative qualified to assist you in the use of such plant and that the terrain is suitable to ensure the plant can be used safely.

Check whether you need any specific training or a permit to work to enter the areas of the site you intend to visit, as these may be required for high risk activities. For example, work in a confined space such as a culvert or sewer will be subject to management controls.

## 1.3 Site occupation and vacant sites

Ascertain from the site owner whether the site is occupied and, if so, whether the occupants need to be informed of, or consent to, your visit.

Consider if children or vulnerable young adults may be present on the site you are visiting. If they are, it is worth checking whether any consents, permissions or DBS (Disclosure and Barring Service)[2] checks are required prior to attending and if the client has a Safeguarding Policy for you to adhere to. If you are visiting an occupied healthcare facility, find out what infection control procedures are in place and make sure you comply with them.

If the site is occupied, determine who is responsible for control of the site and whether there are any specific instructions that you need to be aware of before your visit, including details of any managed emergency evacuation procedures.

Always consider the risk of illegal occupation of vacant sites. Squatters may have caused damage intended to compromise safe access/egress or may have taken measures to prevent eviction that make it unsafe for you to visit. If you suspect this to be the case, avoid entering the site and inform the site owner. Illegally occupied sites may also pose a risk with respect to past or present illegal or illicit activity. For example,

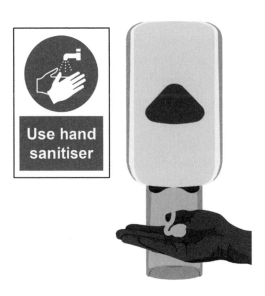

Make sure you comply with any infection control procedures in place at the site you are visiting

toxic residues from drugs manufacturing or discarded needles from intravenous drug use pose a risk of poisoning, infection and/or injury.

## 1.4 Clothing, equipment and personal protective equipment (PPE)

Before leaving for site, enquire about the general site conditions and check the weather forecast to ensure you are dressed appropriately. Ensure you wear sensible and well-fitting footwear and clothing.

Avoid loose-fitting clothes that may snag or get caught on overgrown vegetation or projections.

Wear full-length sleeves and trousers to minimise exposed areas of skin that will be vulnerable to cuts, scrapes and infection. Your footwear should be appropriate for the site conditions. If you are visiting an unoccupied or construction site where there is a risk of debris on the floor that could otherwise injure, you must always wear site boots with a steel soleplate and toecap.

Ensure you are dressed appropriately for the site you are visiting and the activities you plan to undertake whilst there

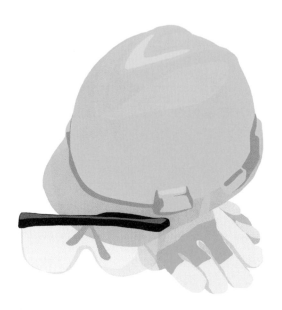

PPE you may require for a site visit includes a hard hat, safety gloves and safety goggles

Consider whether you need to wear protective gloves and/or any head and eye protection, particularly on semi-derelict sites where there might be a risk of dust, contamination or loose falling debris, or on exposed sites where you may be working outside for an extended period of time.

Remember that overexposure to hot, sunny weather can be as much of a risk to your safety and well-being as cold or inclement weather.

If you are visiting an occupied site, check beforehand if there are any requirements for personal protective equipment (PPE) or specialist clothing and whether this will be provided for you on site. If you are required to wear specialist protective clothing that is supplied for you, check that it is in good condition, that it fits you properly and that you are wearing it correctly before commencing work on site. Do not use PPE that appears to have been damaged, altered, tampered with or repaired.

Unless you are in a designated safe area (for example, the site office), the PPE you should wear at all times when visiting a demolition or construction site should include:

Ensure any PPE you require is in good condition and fits you properly

- boots/shoes, with ankle support and a protective midsole and toecap
- a hard hat
- hi-vis clothing
- safety gloves
- eye or hearing protection, if appropriate.

If you are in any doubt about what PPE is required, seek the advice of the person responsible for control of the site before entering any active work areas.

Your employer has a legal duty to provide you with the PPE that you require to undertake your site visit safely and you should not commence your visit without it. Often a contractor will have a supply of PPE that you may use, but this may not always be the case or the PPE available may not be an appropriate size or fit.

Check with the person responsible for control of the site prior to your visit exactly what PPE will be available to you, so you know whether your employer will need to provide you with the necessary PPE instead.

Check that you are wearing any PPE correctly. Ensure your hard hat is fitted square on your head, is not loose and does not obstruct your vision.

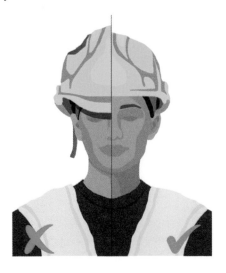

Ensure you are wearing any PPE correctly. Your hard hat should be fitted square on your head

If hazardous activities cannot be postponed during your visit, ensure you have the correct PPE for protection

If you drop your hard hat from height on to a hard surface, notify the person responsible for control of the site and replace it.

Some PPE may be task-specific, for example, different safety gloves protect against different types of hazards. If you are unsure whether the PPE you have is suitable, confirm with the person responsible for control of the site prior to proceeding.

If you observe a particular hazard on site for which you are not adequately equipped and it is not possible to avoid the hazard, return to the site office to obtain the correct PPE. For example, if you are required to visit an area of the site where site personnel are cutting materials and there is a risk of flying debris, ensure you are equipped with impact-rated goggles if the work cannot be stopped briefly to allow you safe access.

Before leaving for site, make sure you have a fully charged mobile telephone and that an appropriate person has the telephone number so they can contact you in the event of an emergency (see Chapter 2 for more detail). Keep your mobile telephone switched on for the duration of your visit with the ring tone volume set to an audible level to ensure that you can hear it. Where the mobile telephone signal strength may be unreliable, identify areas on or close to the site where a sufficiently strong signal is available in case you need to make an emergency call.

Depending on the time of year and conditions on site, consider whether you need to take a torch with you. If you do, check that it is in good working order and either use a wind-up torch or ensure that the batteries are fully charged.

When visiting a remote site, take a bottle of water with you and, if necessary, food and any other provisions.

## 1.5 Weather conditions

It is important that you check the weather forecast and consider recent weather conditions before going on site. Bear in mind that peak flows in streams and rivers may not occur until several hours and possibly days after heavy rain, and can cause unexpected flooding during otherwise benign weather conditions. Inclement weather will also create hazardous working conditions on open or derelict sites and may increase the risk of subsidence and collapse of unstable structures and landscape features.

## 1.6 First aid

Cover any cuts, abrasions or other breaks in the skin with waterproof dressings before you go to site. Equip yourself with a basic first aid kit which may include guidance on first aid, individually wrapped sterile plasters, eye pads and triangular bandages, safety pins, unmedicated wound dressings, disposable gloves, hand sanitiser and anti-bacterial wipes.

If you suffer from any cuts or abrasions whilst on site, cover them with a waterproof dressing as soon as you can and ensure that you wash, disinfect and re-dress them at the earliest opportunity once you have returned from site.

If you have any medical conditions, such as diabetes or severe allergies, consider whether you need to take any medicine with you in case you are on site longer than anticipated. Judge whether any personal conditions may impact or limit your ability to inspect site and adapt your work plan to suit. If you are claustrophobic or suffer vertigo, ensure you advise those accompanying you on your visit and avoid situations that may cause you unnecessary stress or distraction.

Equip yourself with a basic first aid kit

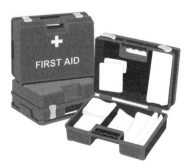

# CHAPTER 2:
# UNDERTAKING SITE VISITS

When you visit any site, you have a responsibility to be mindful of your own safety and that of others who may be accompanying you on your visit or might otherwise be in attendance whilst you are there. Irrespective of whether you have never visited a site before or have many years' experience, you always need to be alert to unexpected or unanticipated hazards so you are ready to act appropriately.

Never be complacent or take your own safety for granted. If you do, you are more likely to make inappropriate decisions that may put you and your colleagues in danger, including those that you may need to call upon to help you in the event of an accident or emergency.

Never take unnecessary risks. If you are in any doubt about whether it is safe to proceed or continue with your site visit, do not do so. If a situation feels unsafe, it probably is, and you should remove yourself from it.

If you are an employer, or are otherwise responsible for supervising a colleague, you have a duty to ensure that those working under your supervision are not exposed to potentially hazardous situations. Make sure employees and colleagues understand the need and feel confident to raise concerns if they come under pressure or feel they are expected to take risks whilst on site, possibly to satisfy a client or contractor or to fit in on sites where the culture around health, safety and well-being might fall short of good practice or may be in breach of health and safety legislation.

Never visit a site if you are under the influence of alcohol or drugs, including prescription medication that may impair your cognitive functions.

In this chapter, we consider 12 aspects regarding how you should conduct your site visit, whether to an unoccupied or occupied site, to ensure you are able to undertake your visit safely:

2.1   Lone working
2.2   Personal site safety

Avoid visiting sites alone, particularly remote, vacant or unoccupied sites

## 2.1 Lone working

Whenever possible, avoid visiting sites alone, particularly remote, vacant or unoccupied sites. If lone working is unavoidable, consider the following precautions prior to undertaking your visit.

- Always identify someone who is willing and able to be your emergency point of contact during your site visit, ensuring that they will be contactable for the duration of your visit.
- Provide your emergency contact with details of your site visit, including its address, your contact mobile telephone number, when you anticipate arriving and how long you expect to be on site.
- Follow this up by confirming when you have arrived on site, any change to your anticipated departure time and then again to confirm when you have left site.

## 2.2 Personal site safety

When you arrive on site, carry out an initial assessment of the site conditions to confirm whether there are any significant hazards or unexpected site conditions that you did not identify from your pre-visit site research and which may have an impact on your proposed plan of work.

Remain vigilant
to any change in
circumstances that
may compromise your
access to and from site

Identify the main site access routes and entrance and exit points, particularly those in the vicinity of the area(s) in which you will be working, so you know where to go in the event of any emergency. Remain vigilant to any change in circumstances that may compromise your access to and from site. For example, if you are working in the vicinity of any livestock, particularly cattle, regularly check that you are not disturbing them and that they do not block your site access.

## 2.3 Person responsible for control of the site

Prior to your visit, ascertain whether the site is unoccupied or occupied and establish who is responsible for control of the site. Ensure you have their permission to access all the areas of the site you intend to visit, including details of any security arrangements, particularly for unoccupied sites. Exchange contact details and emergency contact telephone numbers with the person responsible for control of the site. For demolition and construction sites this will be the principal contractor's site manager or site agent.

Agree the purpose of your visit with the person responsible for control of the site, as well as your anticipated plan of work and what requirements/ provisions need to be in place to enable you to carry out your work safely. Check whether you need to undertake any specialist training or certification before going on site. For example, if you are working adjacent to live transport infrastructure you may require specific training and certification to ensure you are aware of the particular hazards and precautions that this work may involve.

The person responsible for control of the site is legally responsible for all health and safety matters on site and should be your first point of contact for all queries and concerns whilst you are on site.

## 2.4 Induction and orientation

When you arrive on an occupied site, identify and present yourself to the person responsible for control of the site and sign-in.

If it is your first visit to the site, ensure you receive a site induction. This will identity site-specific hazards and the site safety and emergency procedures you are required to follow, the use and type of PPE, location of welfare facilities and where to obtain first aid, if required.

If you have visited the site previously, confirm with the person responsible for control of the site the current status of any site works and whether there have been any changes to the induction information with which you need to familiarise yourself. Bear in mind that the site hazards that you need to be aware of during each visit may change as site work progresses.

Re-confirm with the person responsible for control of the site your proposed plan of work and the areas of the site you intend to visit. Ensure you are aware of any areas to which your access is restricted or

Ensure you are aware of and understand the implications of any particular hazards you are likely to encounter on your site visit

A site that is tidy and well-organised is likely to be well-run and safe

A tidy site is a safe site

Familiarise yourself
with all site safety
information when you
arrive on site

prohibited. Do not enter these areas unless you have express permission to do so.

As a rule of thumb, a site that is tidy and well-organised is likely to be well-run and safe.

If you have any concerns regarding the site management and safety of a site, do not proceed with your visit. Raise any concerns with the person responsible for control of the site and/or site owner, if appropriate, and request that your concerns are addressed before you re-visit the site.

## 2.5 Safety signage

A well-managed site will have relevant site safety notices and information updated on a daily basis available for inspection on notice boards adjacent to the site entrance, site office, welfare facilities, and in the immediate vicinity of the work being carried out.

Familiarise yourself
with current site safety
information at the outset
of each visit and as you
navigate around site

Larger sites may have safety information, including current work activities, located local to areas of the site, for example, at the entrance to each storey. Familiarise yourself with the relevant information at the outset of each visit and as you navigate around the site.

Before going on site, you need to understand the different types of safety signage that you are likely to encounter:

- **Circular red and white signs with a diagonal line are prohibition signs**. These mean you must not do something. For example, do not use your mobile telephone.
- **Circular blue and white signs are mandatory signs**. These mean that you must do something. For example, wear safety gloves or eye protection.
- **Triangular yellow and black signs are warning signs**. These alert you to hazards or danger. For example, warning you a substance or contents are harmful or flammable or that industrial vehicles are in operation.
- **Rectilinear green and white signs are safety signs**. These provide you with safety information. For example, identifying an emergency assembly point, fire exit or first aid station.
- See Appendix 2 for more examples of site safety signs.

## 2.6 Navigating around site

Do not walk and talk whilst you are on site. If you need to make or take a telephone call, make sure you find a safe place to do so and remain stationary until you have finished your conversation. Likewise, do not walk around when you are referring to or making any notes or survey information, including sketching, taking photographs or filming. Do not step or walk backwards.

Make sure you keep your hands free at all times whilst moving around site and remain vigilant, observing site conditions above, beside and in front of you. Do not limit your attention to the floor or areas immediately in front of you.

Circular red and
white signs with a
diagonal line are
prohibition signs

Circular blue and
white signs are
mandatory signs

Triangular yellow
and black signs
are warning signs

Rectilinear green
and white signs
are safety signs

Do not walk around when you are referring to or making any notes or survey information

Do not hurry your visit or rush around. Take your time and try to anticipate or react in a timely fashion to any potential hazards if they occur. Do not proceed and do not take unnecessary risks if in doubt. It is safer to return to site when you have more time or when site conditions improve than to rush to finish your work, risking an accident.

## 2.7 Site vehicles and mobile plant

When you arrive on site, familiarise yourself with the safe pedestrian routes around the site. Bear in mind that these may have changed since your last visit. On a well-managed site, vehicular and pedestrian routes will be segregated by physical barriers. Keep to the designated pedestrian routes at all times and do not attempt to remove, move or circumnavigate any route barriers.

Whilst walking around site, avoid any routes that take you through vehicle compounds or in close proximity to mobile plant that is in use. Mobile plant that is reversing poses the greatest hazard to pedestrians on construction sites. If a vehicle marshal is present, always follow their instructions and heed their warnings. If you are asked to assist marshal mobile plant operations, always politely refuse and avoid the temptation to be helpful. Only trained operatives should marshal mobile plant operations.

If you see a mobile crane lifting a load that is about to hit something, warn the person supervising the lift. If you think a load is about to fall from a moving forklift truck, keep clear but try to warn the driver and others in the area. Never walk underneath a raised load.

Never ride in or on mobile plant, unless it is designed to carry passengers.

Always follow a vehicle marshal's instructions and heed their warnings

Keep to the dedicated pedestrian routes at all times

PEDESTRIAN ROUTE

Never walk underneath
a raised load

If you see mobile plant being driven too fast or operated unsafely, keep out of its way and report the matter to the person responsible for control of the site.

Speak to the person responsible for control of the site to confirm whether it is safe for you to visit areas where site operatives are working

## 2.8 Inspecting construction work

Prepare in advance for your site inspection, including identifying what you intend to inspect and for what purpose. Speak to the person responsible for control of the site to make sure you will have safe access to the areas you require, that the relevant works are ready for your inspection and what special access equipment you will need access to, if any, including suitable PPE for the areas in which you will be working.

Once on site, keep to your proposed plan of work. Avoid distractions and do not allow yourself to be sidetracked during the course of your inspection. If the contractor requires your advice regarding any design or site queries, make time to address these before or after your planned inspection work.

Make a note of any specific health and safety notices applicable to the areas you are inspecting, the relevant fire alarm points and escape routes. This is particularly important during the early construction stages of a project before the permanent fire detection, protection and separation works are complete.

If site operatives are working in the area that you intend to inspect, speak to the person responsible for control of the site to confirm whether it is safe for you to proceed. If hazardous work is being undertaken, including hot works, noisy works or work that is generating dust, postpone your inspection and re-arrange it for a time when the works will have been completed.

Do not continue your inspection or walk around whilst you make notes or sketches and take photographs. Pay particular attention to observing materials, equipment or incomplete or temporary work that could be a potential trip hazard or limit your access. Be mindful that dust and site contamination will limit or reduce the slip resistance of floor finishes and inadequately illuminated spaces can pose hazards and should be avoided.

**Permit to work must be obtained**

Do not enter any restricted areas unless you have permission and appropriate training to do so

Keep to designated safe routes and do not enter any restricted areas, or areas requiring a permit to work, unless you have received permission and/or appropriate training to do so.

If temporary works, materials or equipment restrict your access, do not attempt to move or adapt them. Speak to the person responsible for control of the site and arrange to have the obstruction removed or arrange to carry out your inspection at another time when it will be safe to do so.

If you require access to work at height, check that any ladder, scaffold, access platform or mobile equipment you use is in good condition. If you are required to utilise a fall restraint system, ensure that it is a fall prevention system rather than a fall arrest system (i.e. the harness and lanyard prevent you from falling from height in the first place rather than arresting your fall mid-drop). Being suspended in a fall arrest harness can result in physical trauma, which can be fatal in as little as 15 minutes.

If a fall arrest system is being used and you cannot avoid its use, make sure in advance that:

- the system has been suitability assessed for your intended use
- you receive adequate training in the use of the proposed system

- the equipment is in good working condition
- there is an adequate rescue plan in place in the event that you do fall from height.

Do not proceed unless you are happy it is safe to do so and do not use specialist access equipment unless you have been specifically trained to do so or are using it under adequate supervision.

## 2.9 Communication with site personnel

The principal contractor's site manager or site agent responsible for control of the site should be your primary point of contact whilst you are on site. If you witness any unsafe behaviour by site personnel or hazardous conditions during your visit, notify the site manager before you leave site. Do not instruct site personnel directly, unless you need to alert them to immediate danger.

Do not instruct site operatives directly unless you need to alert them to immediate danger

If you are concerned regarding the safe management of the site by the site manager, notify the principal contractor and/or site owner as soon as it is practical to do so. If your concerns are not addressed, consider whether you should notify the Health and Safety Executive (HSE), particularly if the site poses an imminent risk to the public or to the safety of the site personnel.

Do not respond to queries regarding your design or the works that may be addressed to you directly from site personnel. Ask that all queries are directed via the principal contractor and/or site manager.

Wherever possible, avoid responding to site queries until you have had a chance to properly review and consider the nature of the query, in particular the design risk management implications and potential safety impacts relating to any proposed variations and any knock-on effects to your design.

## 2.10 Site behaviour

Obey the site signs, rules and instructions at all times. Do not imitate bad, irresponsible or unsafe behaviour. Do not proceed with your visit if you are in any doubt about whether it is safe to do so and seek advice from the person responsible for control of the site. Do not proceed with your visit if you experience uncooperative and/or coercive behaviour from any site personnel or the person responsible for control of the site.

## 2.11 Action in the event of an emergency

If you have an accident or find yourself in a dangerous situation, try to remain calm. If possible, attempt to reach a place of safety away from immediate or imminent danger and then raise the alarm or attempt to contact help as soon as you are able.

Take time to assess your situation and to consider the best course of action. If you are on site with colleagues, stay together unless it would be

Ensure that any site services you have used are turned off or isolated before you leave site

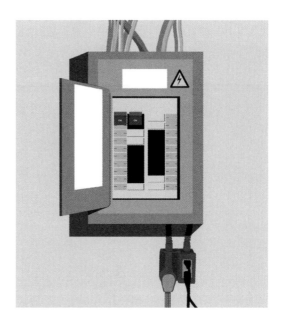

unsafe to do so. Do not take any unnecessary risks with respect to your own or others' safety, and prioritise your personal safety (i.e. abandon any survey equipment, notes or other similar property).

As soon as it is safe to do so, contact the emergency services and/or your emergency point of contact.

## 2.12 Post site visit activity

Before you leave site, check that any access equipment you have used is properly stored and secured to prevent unauthorised use. If you have made use of any site services, ensure that these are turned-off or isolated, as appropriate.

As you leave, check that all access points are adequately secured after you to avoid unauthorised access and notify the person responsible for control of the site that you are leaving. If you have visited a site alone, do not forget to notify your emergency contact that you have left the site.

Check that all access points are adequately secured when you leave site

Once you get back, ensure you wash your hands before consuming any food or drink. Change out of any soiled clothes and ensure they are washed as soon as possible, and certainly before being used again. Do not store muddy or damp site clothes in cupboards or drawers where they could contaminate other clothing or could decay.

Update any site notes and survey information records to include details of any site features or hazards that you have observed during your site visit that have not otherwise been recorded. Pass on relevant details of any hazards or any concerns you have regarding the site to the site owner and notify any colleagues as appropriate.

Prepare written records of any areas of concern that you noted whilst on site, including photographic evidence where possible.

In particular, make a note of any concerns you may have regarding any health, safety and well-being issues and ensure these are shared with

Ensure any PPE you have used is cleaned and stored appropriately

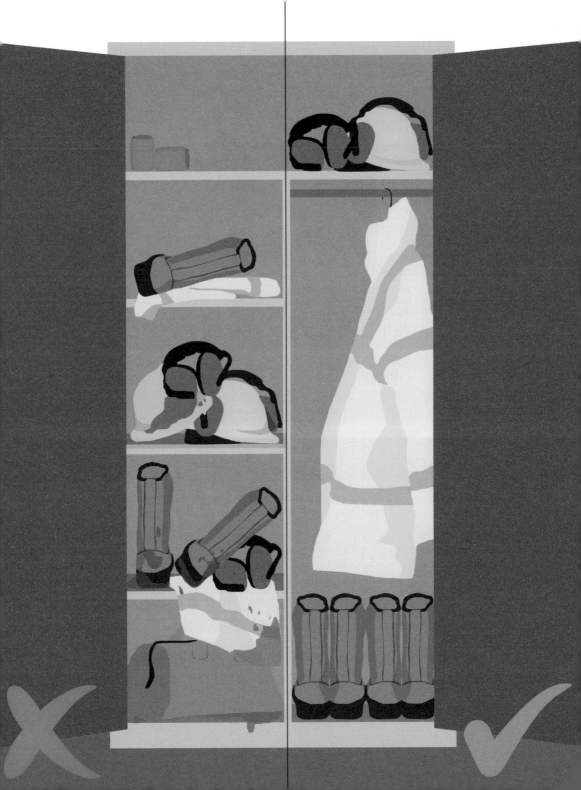

# PER
architects

10 Covent Road
London UK
SW1P 4DJ

tel +44 20 7932 8200
fax +44 20 7932 8201
architects@per.co.uk
www.per.co.uk

## Site Inspection Record – Issue 01.07.19

| Job No: | 10343 | | Project: | Margate Wood |
|---------|-------|--|----------|--------------|
| Notice No: | 00 | Rev: 01 | Contractor: | HCD |
| Inspection Date: | 25.06.19 | | Issued to: | HCD |
| Notice Date: | | | Issued by: | EPR Architects |

| 14 Location: **No.1 all floors** | 25.06.19 |
|---|---|
| Observation: <br> Door handle specification | 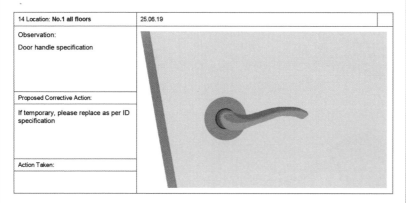 |
| Proposed Corrective Action: <br> If temporary, please replace as per ID specification | |
| Action Taken: | |

| 6 Location: **No.1 All floors** | 25.06.19 |
|---|---|
| Observation: <br> Cork exposed. |  |
| Proposed Corrective Action: <br> Stain cork colour to match adjacent timber flooring. GC to provide mock up for EPR approval. | |
| Action Taken: | |

Distribution
Employer [x] Employer's Agent [x]   Contractor [x] Quantity Surveyor [ ] Struct'l Engineer [x]   File [x]   Other [x]

tel +44 20 7932 8200
fax +44 20 7932 8201
architects@per.co.uk
www.per.co.uk

Distribution
Employer [x] Employer's Agent [x]   Contractor [x] Quantity Surveyor [ ] Struct'l Engineer [x]   File [x]   Other [x]

the site owner, contractor (including the principal contractor) and project team, as appropriate.

Make a written record of any queries raised by the contractor whilst you were on site. If you provided a response whilst still on site, review the advice you gave and confirm details in writing, particularly noting any change in your advice that may be necessary once you have reviewed your position.

If any variations to the project design are required as a consequence of your visit, carry out a design risk management review of the proposed variation. Take into account whether the variation will have any detrimental impact on safety strategies adopted more generally for the design of the project as part of your design risk management strategy, which are considered in more detail in Chapter 4.

# CHAPTER 3:
# SITE
# HAZARDS

Every site is unique. It can be:

- a remote rural location
- a greenfield site
- a brownfield site
- a disused industrial unit
- an unoccupied or occupied office building
- an ancient castle or ruin, or
- a demolition or construction site.

Each will pose unique hazards that you need to consider and manage to ensure you are able to complete your visit safely and return home without incident.

Identifying and providing guidance regarding every possible hazard you may face when visiting site is beyond the scope of this guide.

In this chapter, we consider 15 key aspects regarding the more significant or typical hazards you might face during a site visit and provide guidance on how you can consider managing these to ensure you remain safe:

3.1   Site assessment
3.2   Site contamination
3.3   Falls from height
3.4   Slips and trips
3.5   Unsafe structures
3.6   Excavations
3.7   Enclosed spaces
3.8   Confined spaces
3.9   Respiratory hazards (dust and fumes)
3.10 Noise
3.11 Hazardous substances
3.12 Fire safety
3.13 Manual handling
3.14 Geological, man-made landscape or hydrological features
3.15 Flora and fauna

Each site is unique and will pose unique hazards

## 3.1 Site assessment

When you arrive on site, carry out an initial assessment of the site conditions to confirm whether there are any significant hazards or unexpected site conditions that you did not identify whilst preparing for your visit and which may have an impact on your proposed plan of work.

Start by identifying the main site access routes and entrance and exit points, particularly those in the vicinity of the area(s) in which you will be working, so you know where to go in the event of any emergency. Check that the quality of your mobile telephone reception is adequate. Remain vigilant to any change in circumstances that may compromise your access to, from and around the site.

## 3.2 Site contamination

If you are visiting a building constructed or refurbished before 2000, you need to be particularly mindful of the potential presence of asbestos, which still kills around 5,000 workers each year, more than the number of people killed in road traffic collisions.[1] If you inhale asbestos fibres, which are released into the air when asbestos is disturbed or damaged, you could suffer from fatal and serious lung diseases, including mesothelioma – asbestos-related lung cancer – asbestosis and pleural thickening. There are no immediate symptoms associated with exposure to asbestos and symptoms can take up to 40 years to appear. Once diagnosed, it is often too late to do anything about it. Therefore, it is important to protect yourself during your site visit.

Request and familiarise yourself with the site owner's asbestos register and/or asbestos refurbishment and demolition survey before you visit the site. This will provide you with information on the location, amount and condition of any known or presumed asbestos, particularly any areas where loose asbestos dust or fibres have been identified and to which access should be prohibited. Do not enter prohibited areas unless the site owner can provide you with up-to-date documentary evidence that it is

Familiarise yourself with details of any site contamination before your visit

safe to do so, for example, certification provided by a competent person confirming the area is safe for reoccupation following the removal of the asbestos. If you suspect there is asbestos present on site, particularly loose asbestos fibres, dust or debris, vacate the area immediately, ensuring anyone else in the affected area does likewise and notify the owner of the site. Asbestos encapsulated in products/materials that retain their integrity does not pose a risk if left undisturbed. The HSE must be notified 14 days prior to undertaking any licensed asbestos removal.

Examples of asbestos-containing materials that could pose a hazard include asbestos insulation boards (often found in fire-doors, fire breaks, partitions and fire places), corrugated roofing panels, pipe lagging and gaskets for electrical or mechanical services installations, sprayed structural or fire retardant coatings on steelwork.

Similarly, if you suspect the site is contaminated with any other substances that may be harmful, vacate the area and notify the owner to arrange for sampling and contamination testing. Site contamination can be a particular risk on brownfield, industrial and mining/mineral extraction sites prior to remediation or where slurry or slag materials may have been discarded. Old pipework and paint finishes may contain lead which can be harmful if ingested.

## 3.3 Falls from height

Over the last five years, falls from height have been responsible for 49% of fatal injuries to workers on construction sites,[2] with an average of 36 fatalities to workers and five to members of the public each year over the same time period. The fatal injury rate from falls from height in the construction sector is three times that of all industry rate.

If you need to inspect work at height, it is likely you will need to make use of a scaffold, mobile tower scaffold, temporary working platform or mobile elevating work platform (MEWP). Always ensure that any scaffold or working platform is safe before you access it and check the date on

Ensure any ladder you use is properly secured and in good repair before use

the inspection tag which should be within the past week. If you have any doubts, speak to the site manager who will be able to confirm when the scaffold was last inspected and certified as safe for use.

If you need to use a ladder to access a scaffold or working platform, ensure that it is secured at the top so that it will not slip and that it extends five rungs or 1m above the stepping-off point (if there is no other alternative firm handhold). A leaning ladder should be secured at an angle of approximately 75 degrees.

Never use a ladder with broken rungs, which is not securely fixed or which is relying on wedges at the bottom or another person to keep it secure.

Once you reach the working platform, ensure that there is adequate edge protection to prevent you falling off. This should include a toe-board, a handrail at a minimum height of 950mm and an intermediate guardrail at 470mm centres.

If you need a mobile tower scaffold to carry out an inspection, confirm with the person responsible for control of the site that:

- it has been erected by a trained, competent and authorised person
- the mobile tower is within the maximum height specified by the manufacturer
- you have been briefed on the safe use of the scaffold.

Once you have gained access to the working platform of the mobile tower, make sure that the access hatch is closed behind you to prevent you, or anyone accompanying you, from falling.

If a scaffold obstructs your inspection, never attempt to modify it yourself. Speak to the person responsible for control of the site who will arrange for a competent person to carry out the necessary modifications.

If you are provided access via a MEWP, confirm with the person responsible for control of the site beforehand whether the ground load-bearing capacity has been assessed and that the MEWP is suitable for the terrain in the area

Ensure you are
adequately briefed prior
to using of any mobile
tower scaffold

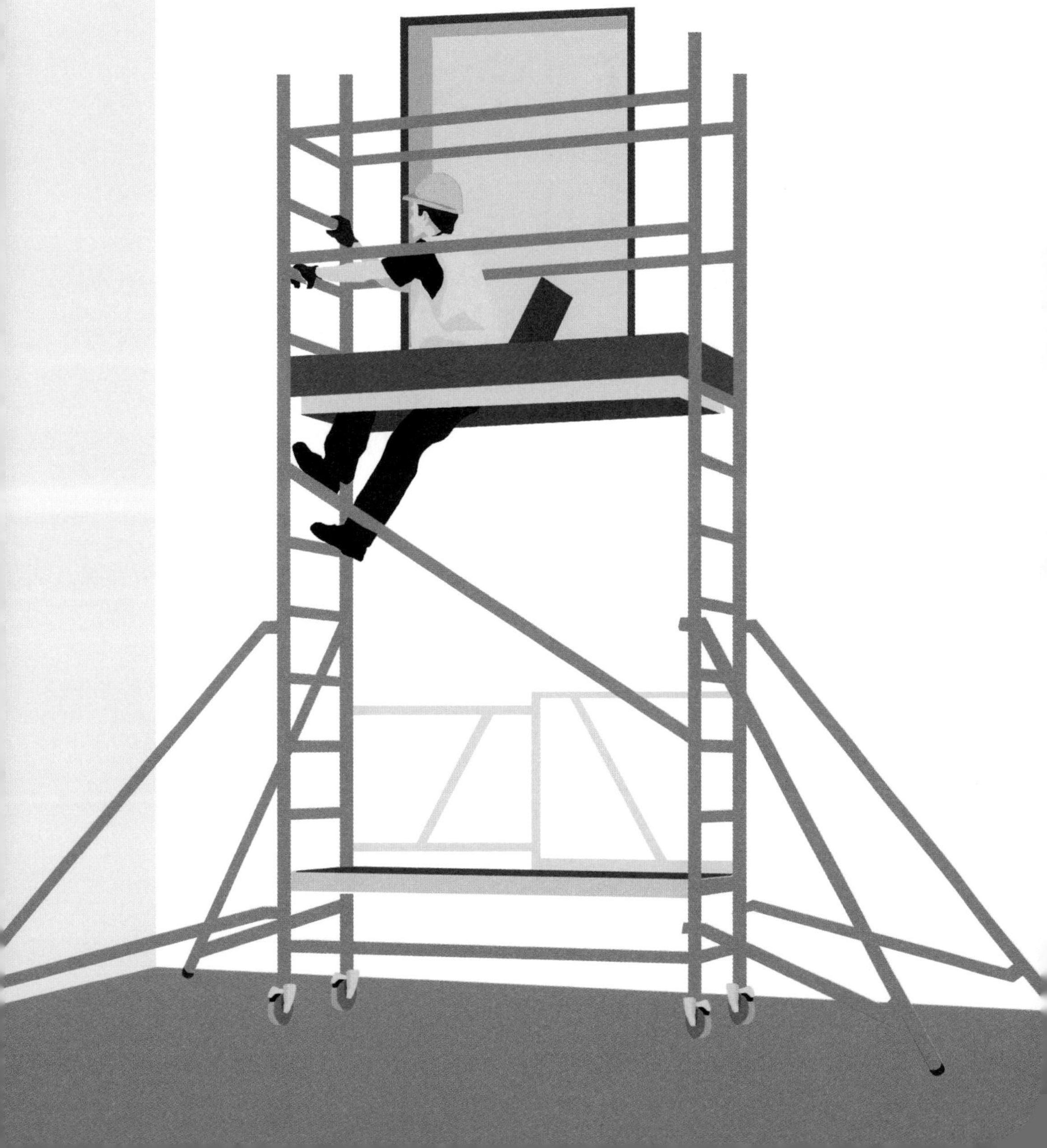

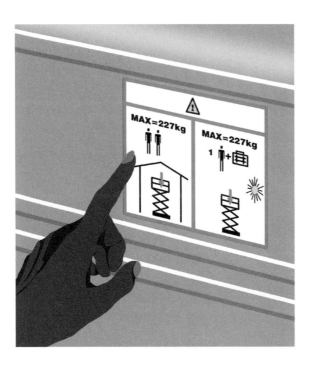

Check the number of people accommpanying you on a MEWP is within the safe working load of the MEWP

of proposed use. This is particularly important on soft ground or where ground may have been disturbed by ground works.

The number of people accompanying you in the MEWP should be within the safe working load, which you should check on the information plate fixed to the MEWP.

Make sure you are provided with an appropriate harness and lanyard before getting on to the MEWP and then attach your lanyard to the designated anchorage point inside the platform before it is elevated. The only exception to this is if you are working over, or near to, deep water to ensure you are not trapped in the MEWP underwater in the event of an accident.

If you need to access a flat roof area, check that it is not a fragile roof or a non-fragile roof with fragile areas (for example, unprotected rooflights, which may be covered in dirt, algae or moss and not clearly visible, or may have not been designed to be walked) or materials that may become

Make sure you are provided with a harness and lanyard before getting on to a MEWP and that this is connected to the anchorage point before elevation

Check all fragile areas of roof are adequately protected before you access the roof

fragile over time that you might fall through. Corrugated asbestos cement roofs are a typical example of a fragile roof that can be a hazard. You should also check that the roof has suitable edge protection and all voids, holes or fragile panels (including roof lights) are protected with secure, load-bearing covers.

## 3.4 Slips and trips

Slips, trips or falls on the same level account for 30% of work-related injuries in the construction sector.[3] Poorly maintained or unmanaged sites pose a risk of an increased likelihood of slips or trips. The presence of contamination by liquids or dust and general site debris increases the risk of slips. Inadequate lighting or uneven floor finishes increase the risk of trips. Exercise caution as you navigate around site, remaining vigilant to any potential slip or trip hazards.

## 3.5 Unsafe structures

Remain vigilant during your visit to the stability and condition of any buildings or structures you may need to enter or work near. Avoid unsafe or fragile structures, for example, floors, stairs and roofs that appear to be in poor condition and any overhead structures through which loose debris may fall. Likewise, avoid working near to unprotected edges where you may fall, including inadequately covered holes, open manholes, maintenance shafts, and structural openings such as lift openings and riser shafts.

If you have concerns about the structural integrity of any areas to which you require access, consider alternative means of access for example, requesting the installation of a temporary working platform or employing drones for visual inspections, remembering to check beforehand if there are any licensing or legal restrictions on drone use.[4] If there are no alternative means of safe access, you should request structural advice is provided before you access those areas.

Check there is adequate light, ventilation and edge protection for the areas of site you intend to visit

Do not enter areas with limited access or areas where you cannot readily determine that the conditions are safe to do so.

Check that there is sufficient light, ventilation and edge protection. Avoid restricted spaces and areas where there is a risk you may be trapped. Check that any doors or gates providing access to the areas where you need to work can be opened from the side you are working on to avoid being locked in.

## 3.6 Excavations

As a general precaution, avoid entering any deep excavations, as these can pose a particular risk of falls from height or burial if they are unstable or are inadequately supported. Consider whether the information you require could be obtained remotely or by alternative means. Do not approach unfenced excavations.

Check that the sides of any excavation you are require to inspect are adequately supported

If it is necessary for you enter a deep excavation, ask the person in control of the site to carry out an appropriate gas detection test beforehand. If you feel unwell whilst inspecting an excavation, leave the area immediately and notify the person in control of the site.

Before you enter an excavation, check that the sides of any excavation you may be required to inspect are battered back, stepped or shored if there is a risk of the sides falling in, regardless of depth.

The site manager should prevent site vehicles from operating in the vicinity of, or approaching any, open excavations to avoid the risk of damage or collapse. If you see vehicles approaching an excavation where there are no stop blocks, or similar measures in place to prevent vehicles getting close to the edge of the excavation, immediately warn anyone working in the excavation and report the matter to the site manager.

Leave the excavation immediately if there is any sign of movement and advise anyone else working in the excavation to do likewise. Only access the excavation via a fixed staircase or ladder; do not climb the sides of the excavation or use the excavation props to enter or exit the excavation.

Do not enter deep
excavations if you are
working alone

Check that vehicles are prevented from operating in the vicinity of any open excavation you are required to inspect

## 3.7 Enclosed spaces

Cramped spaces pose a risk due to their size or the difficulty posed by working within them. This can result in musculoskeletal injuries or problems with evacuation if you have a fall or injury. A typical example is a small roof or loft space.

Avoid entry to any enclosed spaces unless you are certain it is safe to do so, and you have adequate arrangements in place to deal with an emergency.

## 3.8 Confined spaces

A confined space is a space which is substantially (though not always entirely) enclosed and where there is also an identifiable risk to your health and safety, or such risk is reasonably foreseeable (for example, a lack of oxygen or an accumulation of harmful gases or noxious fumes).

73

Remain vigilant to potential changes in circumstance if you are required to enter a confined space

Typical examples of a confined space include culverts, sewers and storage tanks. However, a confined space is not necessarily enclosed on all sides and may not be small or difficult to work in. Examples include service ducts and risers, enclosed rooms (particularly plant rooms), unventilated or inadequately ventilated rooms and ceiling voids, and deep excavations and trenches. Depending on the nature of a space and the activities taking place within it, the status of the space may change depending on the circumstances. For example, heavy rain may present a foreseeable risk of drowning in a space not usually considered confined.

Some of the potential risks associated with confined spaces include:

- the risk of fire or explosion due to the presence of flammable substances (for example, fumes left in a disused fuel tank or leaks from services that have not been adequately isolated)
- excessive heat
- toxic gas, fumes or vapours and/or oxygen deficiency, both of the latter of which could lead to asphyxia or unconsciousness

- the ingress or presence of liquids or solid materials which can flow and that could drown or submerge you and prevent you from breathing.

Avoid entry to any confined spaces and never do so if you are working alone. If entering a confined space is unavoidable, you must ensure that you have a safe system of work in place beforehand that includes adequate arrangements to deal with any emergency.[5] If you feel unwell whilst inspecting a confined space, leave the space immediately and notify the person responsible for control of the site.

## 3.9 Respiratory hazards (dust and fumes)

Dust-making activities on sites, particularly demolition sites, pose hazards that potentially have long-term consequences for your health if you do not take adequate precautions to protect yourself. Breathing in hazardous dust and fumes is the biggest cause of long-term health issues in the construction industry. Occupational asthma,[6] silicosis[7] (sometimes linked to lung cancer) and chronic obstructive pulmonary disease (COPD)[8] are a few of the conditions that commonly result from prolonged exposure to dust on construction sites.

Activities such as cutting or grinding concrete blocks or roof tiles can release harmful dust into the air. This is a particular risk if the activity is taking place in an enclosed or poorly ventilated space and without the site personnel employing appropriate measures to minimise dust. Site personnel should use wet cutting (i.e. using water to damp down dust) or power tools with a dust extractor or collector for such work.

Exposure to paints or resins that have high levels of solvents can cause headaches, sickness, drowsiness, poor coordination and dermatitis or skin problems.

If there's a risk you will be exposed to harmful dust or fumes, avoid the area. If this isn't possible, arrange for access when work is not being carried out or ask the person responsible for control of the site to equip you with suitable respiratory protection, such as a face mask/respirator.

Avoid exposure to paints or resins that have high levels of solvents

Avoid areas with harmful dust or fumes, or, if this is not possible, make sure you are equipped with suitable respiratory protection

Use hearing protection if you need to work in the vicinity of noisy works

## 3.10 Noise

Exposure to noise can cause temporary hearing loss and may lead to permanent, irreversible damage. If you need to inspect an area of site where noisy construction activities are taking place that cannot be stopped, ask the site manager for hearing protection and use it for the whole time you are in the vicinity of the noisy works.

Hearing protection zones are mandatory for all works exceeding 85dB(A). As a rule of thumb, noise levels from construction activities are likely to be hazardous if you have to raise your voice to be heard when someone is standing two or more metres away from you.

## 3.11 Hazardous substances

Prior to commencing your activities on site, confirm with the person responsible for control of the site whether any hazardous substances may be present in the areas you intend to visit. Substances that are

Avoid contact with any hazardous materials

hazardous to health include chemicals, products containing chemicals, fumes, dust, vapours, mists, nanotechnology, gases and asphyxiating gases and biological agents, including germs that cause disease.

Under the Control of Substances Hazardous to Health (COSHH) Regulations 2002,[9] the person responsible for control of the site has a duty to carry out an assessment of any hazardous materials and implement control measures to minimise the risk of harm associated with these. Whilst you should not be directly involved in the use of COSHH-assessed substances, the person responsible for control of the site ought to advise you of any control measures which may have an impact on your site activities.

Whilst inspecting work on site, avoid contact with wet cement, screed or concrete because it can cause serious chemical burns to your skin. Avoid enclosed spaces with no visible means of ventilation where toxins or noxious vapours may pose a health hazard.

## 3.12 Fire safety

If you discover a fire whilst on site, the first thing you should do is raise the alarm either by activating the fire alarm on an occupied site or contacting the emergency services on an unoccupied site.

If you hear a fire alarm whilst on site, head straight to the nearest assembly point and await further instructions from the person responsible for control of the site.

Unless you are – or someone else is – in immediate danger, do not attempt to tackle a fire on site yourself. Different types of site fires will require different fire extinguishers or equipment. Tackling these should only be done by trained operatives.

Familiarise yourself with the location of your nearest fire and assembly points as you navigate around a site

If you are alerted to a fire, head straight to the nearest assembly point and await further instructions

The most common fire risks on construction sites are uncontrolled hot works and poor housekeeping, leading to a build-up of waste material. If you see conditions on site that you think pose a fire risk, advise the person responsible for control of the site before you leave the site, or sooner if you think there is an imminent danger of fire.

## 3.13 Manual handling

Whilst you are on site, never attempt to lift or move any heavy site materials. If you find your access is restricted by site materials, speak to the person responsible for control of the site about making appropriate arrangements to remove the obstruction.

Alert the person responsible for control of the site if you witness uncontrolled hot works being carried out on site

Stay alert to the hazard posed by redundant or concealed site features

## 3.14 Geological, man-made landscape or hydrological features

Typical examples include redundant or historic excavations, wells, sink holes or mine shafts and partially filled or concealed basements. Not being aware of your surroundings, or features masked by undergrowth, can lead to life threating falls.

Deep or fast flowing water can be dangerous, particularly following poor weather conditions and if concealed by overgrown vegetation or adjacent to steep embankments, where the risk of falling in and not getting out unaided may be greater, which could lead to drowning.

If you are exposed to soil or freshwater (such as from a river, canal or lake) and it gets into your mouth, eyes or a cut, you are at risk of contracting leptospirosis[10] (also call Weil's disease). This is an infection you can also

Avoid contact with soil, wildlife and freshwater

catch from animals, typically from the urine of rats and mice, but also cows, pigs and dogs. Whilst leptospirosis is rare in the UK, there is a higher risk of you being exposed to it where there is evidence of rat infestation and when adjacent to canals, rivers and sewers.

The disease starts with flu-like symptoms such as a headache or muscle pains. More severe cases can lead to meningitis, kidney failure and other serious conditions. In rare cases the disease can be fatal.[11] You can reduce your chances of catching leptospirosis by ensuring you avoid coming in to contact with any dead animals or sources of fresh water whilst on site and by exercising good basic hygiene, particularly avoiding hand to mouth/eye contact whilst on site and until you have been able to wash your hands.

## 3.15 Flora and fauna

Take care on unoccupied sites that are poorly managed and where access may be restricted due to overgrown vegetation. Typical risks will include

Avoid contact with giant hogweed

stings, rashes and pricks by thorny plants and nettles. More seriously, giant hogweed, a close relative of cow parsley and an invasive species that can reach over 3m in height, has sap that can cause severe skin burns that may result in blistering, boils and scarring. Giant hogweed is widely distributed in the wild, particularly on sites adjacent to infested woodland, heathland or common land.[12]

Nesting or breeding birds and animals can pose a danger, if threatened. Gulls in particular are known to be aggressively territorial and may swoop towards you or defecate or regurgitate food on you to warn you off. If you are the target of a swooping gull, the best defence is to raise your arms to protect your head and then move away. Resist the temptation to wave your arms around to scare a gull off as this could make it more agitated.

Birds carry a number of diseases that can be harmful to humans, usually through exposure to contact with infected birds or more commonly through inhalation of airborne particles from their dried faeces,

Avoid areas with nesting birds. Use your arms to protect your head and vacate the area if you are attacked by gulls

Do not enter enclosed spaces where large numbers of birds may be or have been nesting

Do not enter poorly ventilated enclosed or confined spaces

particularly where large numbers may be or have been nesting. Human infection can result from brief, passing exposure to infected birds or their dried contaminated droppings, and can cause acute respiratory disease.[13]

Other lung diseases, sometimes known as extrinsic allergic alveolitis[14] can develop if you are exposed to microbes, which form mould on vegetable matter in storage, including mouldy straw, hay or grain, particularly in confined spaces such as poorly ventilated buildings where it is likely you could be exposed to inhaling spores and other antigenic material.

Insect stings are a common hazard for which you should be prepared. If you suffer from anaphylaxis or any allergies to insect stings, ensure you have appropriate medication with you and that anyone accompanying you on site knows how to administer your medication if you are unable to do so.

As well as stings, you need to be wary of bites from ticks which can cause Lyme disease, a bacterial infection that causes flu-like symptoms and a circular red rash, that can appear up to three months after being bitten and usually lasts for several weeks. Treatment requires a course of antibiotics and in severe cases may require treatment over several months. Whilst only a small number of ticks are infected with the bacteria that cause Lyme disease, they are found all over the UK. High-risk areas include grassy and wooded areas in southern England and the Scottish Highlands,[15] particularly in areas where deer have been grazing.

Caterpillars of the oak processionary moth, a European species that found its way to the UK in 2006, have hairs that can cause an unpleasant rash, asthma attacks and other allergic reactions if they or their nests are touched.

Bites from spiders in the UK are uncommon, but some native spiders – such as the false widow spider – are capable of giving you a nasty bite, which can cause nausea, vomiting, sweating and dizziness. Seek medical help immediately if you have any severe or worrying symptoms after a spider bite.[16]

Snakes will sometimes bite in self-defence if disturbed, typically if you accidentally step on one. Some snakes are venomous and can inject venom containing toxins as they bite; however, adders are the only venomous snakes found in the wild in the UK.

If you are bitten by a snake, try to remain calm and do not panic. Snake bites in the UK are not usually serious and are only very rarely deadly. However, you should keep the part of your body that has been bitten as still as possible, loosen any restrictive clothing and seek immediate medical attention.[17]

Seek medical attention at the earliest opportunity if you are bitten by a tick

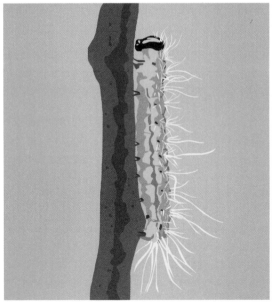

Avoid contact with processionary moths and their nests

If you are bitten by a spider, seek immediate medical attention if you start to exhibit severe symptoms or an allergic reaction

If you are bitten by a snake, loosen restrictive clothing and seek immediate medical attention

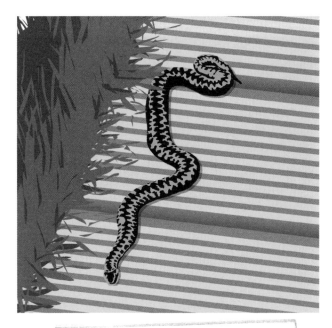

# CHAPTER 4:
# DESIGN RISK MANAGEMENT

Everyone in the design team, including your client, has a duty to work collaboratively to ensure that the buildings we design can be built, occupied, managed, maintained and refurbished or demolished safely.

Architects and lead designers are uniquely placed to influence how effectively safety considerations are embedded in the design process. We have legal, professional and social responsibilities to ensure, so far as is reasonably practicable,[1] that all our projects are well-designed, of good quality, sustainable and safe. We can achieve this by adopting proportionate and integrated approaches to design risk management from the outset of our involvement on every project on which we work.

Much of what we do as architects and designers is learnt by example. This may be from precedent studies of projects by other architects, following the example of colleagues or learning lessons and developing habits based on our own research and experience. However, it is important to avoid repeating the mistakes or shortcomings of past projects or adopting a safety strategy from another project without checking first that it is appropriate to do so. To achieve this, we need to keep abreast of current good practice and understand the safety principles to use as the starting point for each of our projects. This is particularly important, considering the constant evolution of industry benchmarks and standards that aim to raise the bar on what is proportionate good practice with respect to building safety and design risk management.

Some industry commentators advocate a 'safety at all costs' approach. Our role as architects and lead designers requires us to take a balanced approach to building safety and design risk management in the context of the demands and limitations of each project. Whilst the safety aspects of your design are important, these should be dealt with proportionately as each project brief and proposed design develops.

In this chapter, we consider three key aspects of how you do this by understanding and ensuring your design process employs:

## 4.1 Principles of design risk management

There is a misconception by some in our profession that risk management is something separate to the design process and that good risk management requires specialist expertise from someone additional to, and possibly remote from, the design team. Whilst you may need to seek specialist advice in connection with complex projects or to help you to address unusual or unique hazards, you ought to have the competence to manage design risks appropriately for the majority of your projects if you have been appointed as the architect and lead designer.

> Competence can be described as the combination of skills, knowledge and experience that a person has, and their ability to apply them to perform a task safely. Your level of competence should be proportionate to your role and responsibilities. For example, if you are a project architect leading the team you will require a greater level of competence than if you are an architectural assistant working under supervision as part of the design team.

The reality is that we are all experts at risk management. Every action that we take in life from getting out of bed to crossing the road involves an element of risk and therefore risk management. We simply undertake these activities so frequently that we tend to do so subconsciously or without forethought unless or until we are faced with an unusual or particularly challenging situation.

For example, when you want to cross a road the best way to avoid being involved in a road traffic collision is to avoid crossing the road in the first place. However, this may not be a practical or sensible solution if the only way to reach your destination is to cross the road. So before crossing you will undertake a risk management review during which you will decide where, when and how you cross the road. How you do this will depend on your circumstances. How busy is the road? Do you have clear visibility? Are there managed crossing points close by? How much time do you have? You cannot eliminate the risk of being involved in a collision, but you can reduce the risk to an acceptable or tolerable level. There are no hard and fast rules for determining what this acceptable level of risk is and it is likely this will change depending on your circumstances. For example, crossing the road in one location may be acceptable on a quiet Sunday afternoon but less so, or not at all, on a weekday during rush hour.

Design risk management on your projects should be approached in the same fashion. Constructing, occupying, maintaining and cleaning the buildings will always pose risks and eliminating all of these is not practical. For example, work at height and cutting masonry materials pose some of the biggest risks to health, safety and well-being of contractors and maintenance operatives but it is not possible, practical or desirable to avoid these activities in all circumstances. The only way to eliminate all risk would be to not undertake a project in the first place.

Your responsibility as a designer is to review all foreseeable risks with your client and their project team to agree the acceptable level of risk on your project. As with the example of crossing the road, what is acceptable will be unique to the circumstances of each project, depending on your client's priorities and the nature and complexity of the project.

> **Foreseeable risks are hazards that you should anticipate, exercising reasonable skill and care, as the result of your design. For example, personal injury as a result of slips and trips are a foreseeable risk of specifying a highly polished floor finish with a high slip potential in an area accessible to the general public.**

To decide what is acceptable:

Explore options for new technology and innovative design to benefit your design risk management

- consider each risk versus the benefit of managing the risk
- the environment in which the risk is anticipated
- the foreseeable behaviour of people exposed to the risk.

For example, risks that may not be tolerable in a public space may be acceptable in a controlled environment where access is limited to trained operatives with an appropriate level of skill, knowledge and experience to manage the risk.

Good design risk management benefits from diversity of thought.[2] Avoid tick-box, one-size-fits-all type approaches or solutions which inhibit creative thinking or innovative design solutions. If you are faced with a situation you are not sure about, take advantage of the experience and knowledge of others. Treat design risk management as part of the design process and collaborate with the rest of the project team to find the solution most suited to the circumstances of your project.

Do not let design risk management or safety issues limit your design. Exploiting new technology or innovative design can have positive benefits for design risk management. Off-site manufacture, fabrication and assembly are obvious examples of how the construction phase of your project could be better managed or procured to reduce or eliminate some of the hazards associated with on-site construction.

Your duty to do what is reasonably practicable to achieve this end is important. Adopt a proportionate approach to managing risk. When you consider potential hazards, balance the level risk of harm in each case against the measures required to control that risk in terms of money, time and trouble. Also balance this with your other project priorities, for example, your client's budget and programme; your aesthetic aspirations – including any desire to innovate or develop unusual design solutions – and any design decisions that could have environmental consequences. You may not be able to avoid or allow for every eventuality, but by working collaboratively with the rest of your project team you should be able to achieve what is practicable to eliminate or control risks.

Regularly review your design risk management decisions at each stage of your project. The opportunities for eliminating risk through the design will change as the design develops and as your project progresses. Do as much as is reasonable at the time you prepare the design. Do not ignore potential risks at concept design stage, when it is more likely to be reasonably practicable to eliminate them, or you may find you are forced to accept control measures to manage residual risks that compromise the design at the spatial coordination or technical design stage of your project.

When you consider health and safety risks in the context of your other project priorities, it will be inevitable that there will be some hazards and risks that are not reasonably practical for you to eliminate through your design, for example, the need for work at height to clean and maintain your project. In such circumstances, take reasonably practicable steps to reduce or control the risk through your design, employing the principles of prevention, so that harm arising from the risk is less likely or the potential consequences are less serious.

Treat design risk management as part of the design process

Design risk management – the process of deciding which risks you attempt to eliminate, reduce or control – is not always straightforward. Do not rely on a formulaic tick-box approach or duplicate design solutions or strategies taken from previous projects. The context of each of your projects and their associated hazards and risks will be unique. How you respond to this and consider the elimination, reduction or control of risks requires your professional judgement based on your own experience, consultation with your client and advice from the professional team, contractors, specialist suppliers and manufacturers involved in your project.

The imperative to eliminate a risk depends on how significant a risk it is in the context of your project. The more significant a risk, the more effort you should make to eliminate it through your design. Significant risks are not necessarily those that involve the greatest risk but those that may not necessarily be obvious, are unusual or likely to be difficult to manage effectively.

To implement effective design risk management, you need to understand the difference between a hazard and a risk.

**A hazard** is an object or substance, a situation or an activity that has the potential to cause someone harm. For example, a floor without adequate slip resistance is a hazard because slips and trips can cause injuries; loud noise from construction site plant and equipment is a hazard because it can cause temporary or permanent hearing loss; and breathing in asbestos dust is a hazard because it can cause cancer.

**A risk** is the likelihood – that is, the probability or frequency – that a hazard will actually cause someone harm, together with a measure of its effect. For example, a floor without adequate slip resistance is more likely to cause harm in a public space or more serious injury if it is used on a staircase or ramp.

Confirm the slip resistance of a floor finish using independent test data before you specify it

When you are designing your project, think about the changing circumstances in which people may be faced by potential hazards. For example, when designing accessible roofs, think about the hazards and likelihood of harm faced by personnel that need unplanned access to the roof in an emergency on a cold, wet, dark Friday afternoon, as well as those undertaking planned maintenance in more clement conditions.

Some of the hazards that you ought to consider include:

- **Fire** poses a significant hazard, not just once your project is completed but also during the construction phase. Each year there are hundreds of fires on construction sites, putting the lives of site workers and the public at risk. The HSE's publication HSG168 provides guidance on how to reduce the risk of fires on construction sites.[3] The Fire Protection Association (FPA) also provides guidance in their publication 'Fire Prevention on Construction Sites', often referred to as the Joint Fire Code, relevant to the design stage of buildings.

  Your project fire strategy should consider fire safety during the construction phase of the project, in particular measures to reduce and control the risk of fire before the permanent fire safety installations are complete. This is particularly important for buildings where fire spread from the construction site might endanger the lives of people in adjacent properties or buildings that are more vulnerable to fire during the construction phase. Modern methods of construction that rely on component parts that are left temporarily unprotected or exposed once in-situ on site (for example, timber frame or composite buildings panels), may need extra precautions at certain vulnerable times of the build to minimise the risk of fire. Most construction-related fires are the result of flying sparks from hot works that can become trapped in cracks, gaps, holes and other small openings where they can smoulder and cause the outbreak of fire. Specifying systems and materials that negate the need for hot works can contribute significantly to avoiding fires on site. If hot works are necessary, the risk can be managed using temporary fire suppression systems, observing fire watches for an hour following hot works, or having the appropriate fire extinguisher available close by (listed from most to least effective).

Agree the principles of the project fire safety strategy for the permanent works with your client at concept design stage, or as soon as you start work on the project if appointed at a later work stage. As a minimum, the fire safety strategy should address fire safety measures relating to means of warning and escape, external fire spread and access and facilities for the fire service as well as recording all key design decisions relating to fire safety.[4] We look at some of the regulatory requirements and guidance relating to fire safety in Chapter 5.

- **Falls from height** are one of the biggest causes of fatalities and major injuries in our industry. Common cases include falls from ladders and through fragile surfaces. Take a sensible approach to managing this hazard. Equipment to enable working at height should be appropriate for the task undertaken and their associated risks, including temporary scaffolding with a working platform and fixed access ladders for more prolonged work, or the use of a mobile scaffold tower or MEWP, where fixed access is unnecessary. The HSE provides useful guidance regarding some of the dos and don'ts of planning for work at height.[5] Bear in mind there may be some low-risk situations where common sense tells you no particular precautions are necessary.

Take a sensible approach to designing for work at height

- **Musculoskeletal Disorders** (MSDs) include injures and conditions that can affect the back, joints and limbs and effect construction workers more than in any other industry. They are caused by manual handling, repetitive work and awkward postures. You should consider how your design can prevent or minimise the risk of workers developing MSDs, including in particular avoiding or reducing the need for manual handling. The HSE provides useful guidance on musculoskeletal disorders at work[6].

- **Legionella bacteria** can lead to a potentially fatal type of pneumonia called Legionnaires' disease that can be contracted by inhaling airborne water droplets containing the bacteria. Legionella bacteria thrive in stagnant water but are dormant below 20°C and do not survive above 60°C, therefore water should not be stored between these temperatures. Public health systems should be designed to keep pipe work as short and direct as possible with adequate insulation to pipes and tanks, using fittings and materials that prevent contamination and do not encourage the growth of Legionella.

- **Dust**, particularly silica dust, poses the biggest risk to construction workers' respiratory health after asbestos. Silica is a natural substance found in construction materials such as bricks, tiles, concrete and

Develop your design to minimise the need for cutting or working silica construction materials on site

mortar. Cutting, drilling, grinding and polishing materials releases fine particles of silica dust that cause respiratory disease. You can minimise the health risks to workers by considering whether specifying materials containing silica could be avoided or moderated. Often specifying such materials is unavoidable, so develop your design to minimise the need for cutting or working the material on site.[7]

- **Slips and trips** are the most common cause of injury in the workplace and can lead to other accidents, including falls from height. Minimise the risk of slips and trips by specifying floor finishes that have a low slip potential[8] and provide suitable information and advice to your client regarding the cleaning and maintenance regime required to maintain the slip resistance of the floor finish you have specified as dirt or contamination will effect its performance. Over-zealous cleaning and polishing of a floor will reduce its surface roughness and undermine its slip resistance and potential to create a hazard where there was not one before. Confirm the slip resistance of a floor finish before you specify it, using independent test data[9] to confirm the floor's slip potential in both the wet and dry states. Be cautious of relying on applied finishes to achieve an adequate slip resistance for new floors, particularly finishes that will be applied on site, where inadequate quality control and cleaning or maintenance may undermine the required performance of the floor.

- **Temporary works** used to provide provisional support or protection to the permanent works during the construction of your project require correct design and installation/maintenance to prevent and mitigate risks during construction. Whilst responsibility for the design and installation of temporary works may be delegated to a specialist and/or the contractor, you still need to understand and consider the requirement for, and practicality of, employing temporary works. Think about how the permanent works will be constructed and whether these may impact on how any temporary works can be safely constructed and dismantled without compromising your design. Consider whether it may be safer and/or more economical to sacrifice the temporary works and leave them in place following construction of the permanent works, which is often necessary for complex below ground and sub-structure works.

Consider how permanent works will be constructed and the impact this may have on the design, construction and dismantling of any temporary works

Red, amber, green lists (commonly known as RAG lists) provide helpful guidance regarding the nature and type of hazards and risks to consider as part of your design risk management. A RAG list may also be used as a management or control tool by your client, or their principal designer or principal contractor, as part of the safety strategy and as a way of monitoring and communicating details regarding residual risks on your project. Industry guidance for designers produced by the Construction Industry Training Board (CITB) and HSE provides a good example of a RAG list.[10]

The red lists include hazardous procedures, products and processes that you should eliminate from your project, wherever possible. For example, this could include proceeding with your design without adequate pre-construction information, designing glazing that cannot be accessed for cleaning or replaced safely, or designing structures that do not allow for fire safety and containment during construction.

Amber lists include products, processes and procedures to be eliminated or reduced, as far as possible and only specified if unavoidable. Incorporating amber items in your design requires you to provide relevant information to the principal contractor and client regarding any residual risks. Examples of amber items include the specification of heavy building blocks (i.e. blocks in excess of 20kg), designing large and heavy glazing panels, and the specification of solvent-based coatings.

Green lists include products, processes and procedures that you should aim to include in your design. For example, provide edge protection where there is a foreseeable risk of falls from height, design practical and safe methods for window cleaning (such as from the inside), specify floor finishes to minimise the risk of slips and trips during use and maintenance, and design for off-site fabrication and prefabricated elements to minimise site hazards.

Carry out regular reviews of the red, amber and green aspects of your design to consider how to adapt or modify your design to reduce the red and amber elements and increase the green elements. The most effective way to achieve this is to employ the general principles of prevention.

Regularly review your design and employ the general principles of prevention to reduce red and amber procedures, products and processes

## 4.2 General principles of prevention

You have a legal duty under the Management Regulations and the Construction (Design and Management) Regulations 2015 (also known as CDM Regulations) to consider the general principles of prevention as part of your design risk management strategy. The principles of prevention, which apply to all industries, not just construction, provide a framework to identify and implement a proportionate design risk management strategy to control foreseeable risk.

Simply put, you employ the principles of prevention at all stages of your design development, from the beginning of the concept design stage to the completion of the technical design stage, to avoid putting people at risk, i.e. amend a potentially hazardous design to be safer, or less dangerous.

The general principles of prevention, which are specified in Schedule 1 of the Management of Health and Safety at Work Regulations 1999,[11] are:

1.  **Avoid risks**. Consider the potential hazards created by your design and aim to avoid these by making variations to your design. For example, replace areas of fragile roofing with load-bearing or impact-resistant construction to avoid falls from height, and specify pre-formed brick or blockwork to avoid the need for site cutting and exposure to dust.

2.  **Evaluate the risks which cannot be avoided**. Consider the likelihood and severity of harm posed by the hazards that you cannot avoid, determining how much of a risk they pose to the people that will be constructing, maintaining, occupying and demolishing your project. Agree with your client what the tolerable level of risk is in the context of your project. Remember that what is acceptable may vary for different areas of the project, particularly if parts of your project will be accessible to members of the public.

3.  **Combat the risks at source**. Adapt your design to avoid the need for further intervention in the future (for example, design glazing at height so that it can be safely cleaned from inside − specify

reversible windows (with restrictors and/or friction stays) with appropriate guarding or sill heights to deal with the risk of falls from height). Design and specify the layout and size of fixed panes and spandrel panels in accordance with the maximum reach suitable for cleaning and maintenance from inside the building. This will minimise the risk of falls from height and avoid the need for specialist cleaning equipment. Bear in mind the maximum reach may need to include the window frame and sill as well as the glazed area.

4. **Adapt the work to the individual**. This is especially pertinent in the design of workplaces. Agree with your client the choice of work equipment and the choice of working and production methods, with a view to alleviating monotonous work and work at a predetermined work rate to reduce ill effects on the health of workers. Consider the design and specification of construction materials to avoid repetitive, manual handling, for example, specifying a pre-fabricated, panelised wall system instead of large areas of masonry construction.

5. **Adapt to technical progress**. Whilst the basic process of construction has not changed significantly since the Middle Ages, the technical processes and methods used have. Advances in construction technology can improve quality, efficiency, value for money and sustainability as well as safety. BIM (Building Information Modelling) modern methods of construction, modular construction, off-site manufacturing, prefabrication and preassembly, smart technology, robotics, and GPS-controlled equipment are all examples of technology that can be utilised to improve safety on your project.

6. **Replace the dangerous by the non-dangerous or the less dangerous**. Consider the hierarchy of design solutions available to you. For example, when you are agreeing a maintenance strategy with your client, rope access may be discussed as an acceptable solution, but a less dangerous solution would be to design your building to be accessible at every storey by utilising roof terraces or balconies for safe level access and specifying windows that can be cleaned from inside, or by incorporating a building management unit (BMU) into your design.

7. **Develop a coherent overall prevention policy**. Discuss and agree with your client a safety strategy for the project that considers the

Advise your client where appropriate instructions or control measures may need to be identified or implemented by the building users

use of technology, organisation of work, working conditions, social relationships and the influence of factors relating to the working environment.

8. **Give collective protective measures priority over individual protective measures**. Any design solution that protects everyone from harm without the need for them to take any particular action is safer than one that only protects individuals or a small number of people and/or requires those people to undertake special training or a particular action or behaviour to safeguard their safety. Accessible roofs with suitable permanent edge protection provide collective protection to everyone accessing the roof. Roof access that relies on a lanyard or fall prevention safety system for safety will only provide protection to a small number of individuals. A system-based solution will necessarily require access to be restricted to site personnel that have appropriate training to use the particular system specified, and for the system be effective it relies on such site personnel actually making the effort to use it.

9. **Give appropriate instructions to employees**. Ensure that you provide clear, concise and relevant information to all those who may require it regarding any hazards that require a safety management plan.[12]

If during your design development you find it is not reasonably practicable to design-out a risk, despite applying the principles of prevention, provide adequate information regarding the residual risks to ensure that proportionate measures can be taken to control them at source. For example, advise your client where appropriate instructions or control measures may need to be identified or implemented by the building users.

## 4.3 Effective communication and coordination

Effective communication and coordination of your work with your client and their design and construction teams is key to ensuring your project can be constructed, occupied and maintained safely.

Discuss and agree with your client their strategic requirements at the brief and concept stages of your project. Make sure you have documented and agreed project strategies in place from the outset of the project, for example, fire, health and safety, and cleaning and maintenance strategies. If you join a project after completion of the brief or concept design stage, take time to familiarise yourself with your client's brief and existing safety strategies, or prioritise putting these in place if they have not already been agreed.

You need to understand your client's attitude to risk and spend time with them, relative to their knowledge and experience, explaining their duties to ensure they understand how important a client's role is and their potential to positively influence the safety outcomes of the project. If your client lacks experience or appears to have a relaxed attitude to health and safety, you need to take more time to advise them of their legal duties. Ensure that they understand that they need to meet certain standards and explain the potential implications of not doing so; not just the implications for them as a client (for example, prosecution and reputational damage) but also for the project and everyone involved in the project (for example, injury or death of personnel and delays and additional costs to the project).

Deal with design risk management as an integral part of your regular client and design team meetings

Discussing and communicating health and safety matters on your project should not be done separately to the design process. The most effective way to embed design risk management in the design process is to deal with it as part and parcel of client and design team meetings. This encourages regular and effective engagement with the whole design team. If you are appointed as the lead designer or lead design consultant, include regular discussion and information exchanges regarding relevant aspects of design risk management as part of your design coordination.

Deal with health and safety as you would any other aspect of your design development, on an ongoing basis. A design risk management review is not a task to be undertaken, ticked off and then forgotten. As your design develops, new hazards may present themselves or the level of risk posed by existing hazards may change. You need to address this on an ongoing basis and the most efficient and effective way to do this is to develop habitual behaviour amongst your design team to discuss and address hazards and risks as they arise, in a proportionate way, in conjunction with other competing project risks and opportunities.

Take time to produce clear and concise records of your design risk management discussions, including the agreed outcomes. This might be in the form of meeting minutes, annotations on or mark-ups of drawings or digital models, or monthly reports, depending on the approach agreed with your client as part of your agreed health and safety strategy. Whatever is agreed, it is important that all members of the design and construction team take a consistent approach and that records are clear, concise, specific and proportionate to the risks on your project.

If you or your client propose to use a digital strategy, for example, BIM or a project electronic data management system (EDMS), to coordinate and communicate design risk management information, ensure that all members of the design, construction and maintenance teams have the competence and capability to engage effectively with this strategy, including access to and knowledge of the chosen software. A consistent approach to managing health and safety information is crucial to ensuring that all relevant information is available to those who need it and

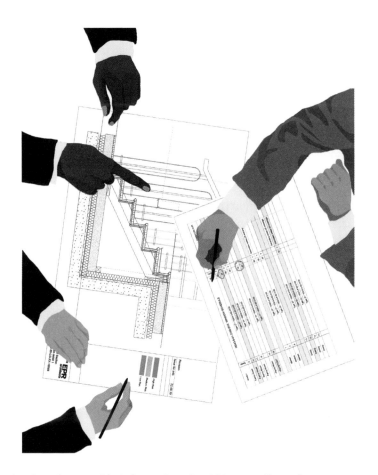

Provide clear and concise information regarding how you have designed-out significant risks

at the time they need it. Information should be coordinated at every stage of your project to ensure that it is all readily available in one place in a single, user-friendly format.

Employing the principles of prevention as part of your design development and approach to design risk management targets the elimination, so far as reasonably practicable, of all foreseeable risks associated with the construction, maintenance, occupation and demolition of your project. Despite this, there will always be risks that it is not possible, practicable or desirable to eliminate, considering your other desired project outcomes.

When you decide to reduce or control a risk, rather than eliminate it inform your client and your client's professional team – including the contractor – regarding the residual risks that remain because of your decision. In doing so, the nature and level of information you provide should be project-specific, clear, concise and proportionate to each risk. Do not use generic schedules or information copied from another of your projects. Whilst reviewing precedents may be helpful to decide what might be suitable in the context of your current project, they should not be taken to confirm the acceptability of your proposals. Do not include irrelevant information that will obscure the important information your client and/or their contractor requires to control the risks specific to your project.

The information you provide should focus on significant or unusual residual risk. Do not provide information regarding insignificant risks or those arising from routine construction activities, of which a competent contractor or building manager ought to be aware. If you do, there is a danger the relevant information could be overlooked.

Carefully consider what information you should provide regarding risks that you have eliminated through your design risk management. Retaining details of your risk assessments for yourself will be useful to record your approach to the design risk management and decision-making process but may be of little value to your client and/or their contractor provided a hazard no longer poses a risk. Provide clear and concise information regarding how you have designed-out significant risks, particularly if responsibility for your design is passed to another designer and/or you are not retained to provide services in connection with your project through to completion. If it is foreseeable that a design variation by others later in the project could re-introduce a significant risk that you have previously eliminated, consider whether it may be appropriate to provide information regarding the positive design decisions you made to help the new design team to evaluate whether circumstances may have changed and whether it is still reasonably practical to eliminate the risk.

# CHAPTER 5: STATUTE, GUIDANCE AND CODES OF CONDUCT

To fulfil our architectural duties professionally we need to understand the current minimum legal requirements, in terms of professional duties and design, imposed by government legislation and codes of conduct. However, be mindful these only provide a benchmark for minimum standards. Good practice and good-quality, sustainable design may require you to exceed statutory minimums.

In this chapter, we consider the standards with which you need to be familiar:

5.1   Statute and the regulatory environment
5.2   Statutory and non-statutory guidance
5.3   Codes of conduct

# 5.1 STATUTE AND THE REGULATORY ENVIRONMENT

We work in a regulated industry with rules that mandate minimum standards and duties regarding how we manage the work we do that has an impact on the health, safety and well-being of others. These statutory rules comprise primary and secondary legislation.

> The extent to which legislation is applicable across the United Kingdom[1] varies. For the purposes of this guide, guidance provided is applicable to England, unless noted otherwise. You should confirm the extent to which legislation is applicable or differs in Wales, Northern Ireland and Scotland prior to undertaking projects in these jurisdictions.

- Primary legislation typically takes the form of an Act of Parliament and is the general term used to describe the main laws passed by the legislative bodies of the UK.

- Secondary legislation is law created by ministers (or other bodies) under powers given to them under the primary legislation. Secondary legislation often takes the form of regulations or statutory instruments.

The two pieces of primary legislation that you need to be familiar with are the Health and Safety at Work etc Act 1974 ('the HSWA')[2] and the Building Act 1984.[3]

The **Health and Safety at Work etc Act** covers occupational health and safety in Great Britain. The Health and Safety Executive ('the HSE') is responsible for enforcing the HSWA, which sets out the general duties employers have towards employees and members of the public, employees have to themselves and to each other, and certain self-employed have towards themselves and others.. The are several regulations that are enacted under the HSWA. Some of those that you need to be familiar with include:

- **The Confined Spaces Regulations 1997**, which define what a confined space is and imposes obligations on employers to protect employees who may be working in confined spaces.
- **The Construction (Design and Management) Regulations 2015** ('the CDM Regulations'), which impose duties on those responsible for the construction process, from concept to completion, to ensure projects are carried out in a way that secures health and safety.
- **The Control of Asbestos Regulations 2012**, which impose a duty to manage asbestos and asbestos-containing materials (ACMs) in non-domestic premises on every person with control over, or an obligation with respect to, maintenance or repair of that premises in order to protect anyone using or working in the building from health risks associated with exposure to asbestos.
- **The Management of Health and Safety at Work Regulations 1999** ('the Management Regulations'), which make explicit requirements for employers to satisfy the requirements of the HSWA.
- **The Manual Handling Operations Regulations 1992** ('the MHOR'), which place obligations on employers to manage the risks of manual handling faced by their employees.

If you are an employer, you are obliged to manage the risks of manual handling faced by your employees

- **The Regulatory Reform (Fire Safety) Order 2005** ('the FSO'), which requires that a responsible person with control of a building takes reasonable steps to reduce the risk from fire and makes sure people can escape safely from a building in the event of a fire.
- **The Work at Height Regulations 2005** ('the WAHR'), which apply to all work at any height (even if it is at or below ground level) where there is a risk of a fall that may cause injury.
- **The Workplace (Health, Safety and Welfare) Regulations 1992**, which encompass a wide range of fundamental health, safety and welfare issues that are applicable to most workplaces, excluding construction sites.

The **Building Act** is intended to secure the health, safety and welfare of people who may use buildings or might otherwise be affected by buildings or matters connected with buildings. Each national jurisdiction sets its own building regulations for building work. In England the **Building Regulations 2010**[4] are enacted under the Building Act and are a set of national building standards that apply to the majority of new buildings and alterations to existing buildings, including projects involving a material change of use.

The primary purpose of the Building Regulations is to ensure that all building work is carried out to a standard that ensures the health and safety of building users, as well as standards for energy conservation, building access and security.

**Regulation 4** '*Requirements relating to building work*' of the Building Regulations makes it a legal requirement that building work is carried out so that it complies with the applicable functional requirements set out in Schedule 1 of the Building Regulations in England.

Schedule 1 is arranged in Parts A to R and each part includes a description of the legal minimum requirement or requirements that building work is required to meet. These requirements must be met either through the design or construction of the building work and are described in terms of function rather than form. This allows you the flexibility to determine the most appropriate design solution for your project that will meet the required function rather than being restricted to the use of a prescribed design solution.

**Schedule 1 of the Building Regulations 2010 (these functional requirements differ slightly in Northern Ireland, Scotland and Wales)**
- **Part A Structure**
  - A1 Loading
  - A2 Ground movement
  - A3 Disproportionate collapse
- **Part B Fire Safety**
  - B1 Means of warning and escape
  - B2 Internal fire spread (linings)
  - B3 Internal fire spread (structure)
  - B4 External fire spread
  - B5 Access and facilities for the fire service
- **Part C Site preparation and resistance to contaminants and moisture**
  - C1 Site preparation and resistance to contaminants
  - C2 Resistance to moisture
- **Part D Toxic substances**
  - D1 Cavity insulation

- **Part E Resistance to the passage of sound**
  - E1 Protection against sound from other parts of the building and adjoining buildings
  - E2 Protection against sound within a dwelling house, etc
  - E3 Reverberation in common internal parts of buildings containing flats or rooms for residential purposes
  - E4 Acoustic conditions in schools
- **Part F Ventilation**
  - F1 Means of ventilation
- **Part G Sanitation, hot water safety and water efficiency**
  - G1 Cold water supply
  - G2 Water efficiency
  - G3 Hot water supply and systems
  - G4 Sanitary conveniences and washing facilities
  - G5 Bathrooms
  - G6 Food preparation areas
- **Part H Drainage and waste disposal**
  - H1 Foul water drainage
  - H2 Wastewater treatment systems and cesspools
  - H3 Rainwater drainage
  - H4 Building over sewers
  - H5 Separate systems of drainage
  - H6 Solid waste storage
- **Part J Combustion appliances and fuel storage systems**
  - J1 Air supply
  - J2 Discharge of products of combustion
  - J3 Warning of release of carbon monoxide
  - J4 Protection of building
  - J5 Provision of information
  - J6 Protection of liquid fuel storage systems
  - J7 Protection against pollution
- **Part K Protection from falling, collision and impact**
  - K1 Stairs, ladders and ramps

- K2 Protection from falling
- K3 Vehicle barriers and loading bays
- K4 Protection from collision with glazing
- K5 Additional provisions for glazing in buildings other than dwellings
- K6 Protection against impact from and trapping by doors
- **Part L Conservation of fuel and power**
  - L1A Conservation of fuel and power in new dwellings
  - L1B Conservation of fuel and power in existing dwellings
  - L2A Conservation of fuel and power in new buildings other than dwellings
  - L2B Conservation of fuel and power in existing buildings other than dwellings
- **Part M Access to and use of buildings**
  - M1 Access and use of buildings other than dwellings
  - M2 Access to extensions to buildings other than dwellings
  - M3 Sanitary conveniences in extensions in buildings other than dwellings
  - M4(1) Category 1: Visitable dwellings
  - M4(2) Category 2: Accessible and adaptable dwellings
  - M4(3) Category 3: Wheelchair user dwellings
- **Part P Electrical safety**
  - P1 Design and installation of electrical installations
- **Part Q Security – Dwellings**
  - Q1 Unauthorised access
- **Part R Physical infrastructure for high-speed electronic communications networks**
  - R1 In-buildings physical infrastructure

Details of the functional requirement for each part can also be found in the green text boxes at the start of each relevant section of the Approved Documents guidance that accompany the Building Regulations.

**Regulation 7** '*Materials and workmanship*' of the Building Regulations makes it a legal requirement that building work shall be carried out with adequate and proper materials which are appropriate for the circumstances in which they are used, are adequately mixed or prepared, and are applied, used or fixed so as to adequately perform the functions for which they are designed, and that building work shall be carried out in a professional manner.

**Regulation 38** '*Fire safety information*' of the Building Regulations applies with respect to building work where Part B of Schedule 1 imposes a requirement in relation to work on a relevant building. The regulation makes it a legal requirement that the person carrying out the work shall give fire safety information to the responsible person not later than the date of completion of the work, or the date of occupation of the building or extension, whichever is the earlier.

A *relevant building* in relation to Regulation 38, is a building to which the Regulatory Reform (Fire Safety) Order 2005 applies or will apply after completion of building work. This generally means any building that is or may be a workplace, excluding domestic premises.

*Fire safety information* means information relating to the design and construction of the building or extension, and the services, fittings and equipment provided in, or in connection with, the building or extension which will assist the responsible person to operate and maintain the building or extension with reasonable safety.

The *responsible person* means in relation to a workplace, the employer, if the workplace is to any extent under the employer's control; in relation to any other premises the person who has control of the premises (as occupier or otherwise) in connection with the carrying on by that person of a trade, business or other undertaking (for profit or not); or the owner, where the person in control of the premises does not have control in connection with the carrying on by the person of a trade, business or other undertaking.[5]

# 5.2 Statutory and non-statutory guidance

Various government agencies and industry bodies produce approved codes of practice, standards and other guidance that provide advice to help you to understand your legal duties and how you might discharge those duties, either through the design of your project or your actions as an employee and/or employer. This guidance may be statutory or non-statutory, either way it does not have any legal status and it is not compulsory to follow the recommendations contained in it. However, if you do follow the guidance you will normally be doing enough to comply with the law.

Examples of statutory and non-statutory documents that provide guidance regarding how you might discharge your duties under the primary and secondary legislation include:

**Approved Documents**,[6] which are published by the government and provide statutory guidance on ways to meet the functional requirements of the Building Regulations. The documents contain general guidance on the performance expected of materials and building work to comply with the Building Regulations as well as practical examples and solutions on how to achieve compliance for some of the more common building situations. There is an Approved Document for each of the parts of Schedule 1 of the Building Regulations, as well as an Approved Document providing guidance regarding material and workmanship to comply with Regulation 7. The guidance in the Approved Documents is informative only. You may employ an alternative means of satisfying the minimum requirements of the Building Regulations, for example, by designing your building in accordance with the guidance in relevant British or European Standards.

**British and European Standards**[7] contain non-statutory guidance produced by, for and on behalf of industry and are published by the British Standards Institute (BSI). Following the guidance in these standards is one way to demonstrate that you have discharged your statutory duties. For example, guidance in relevant standards may be used as an alternative to the Approved Documents to demonstrate compliance with the functional

Approved Documents A to R provide statutory guidance on ways to meet the functional requirements of the Building Regulations

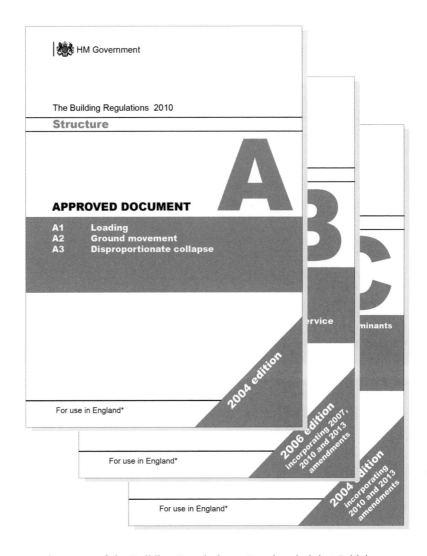

requirements of the Building Regulations. Bear in mind that British Standards take the form of guidance and recommendations, which you need to take the time to understand to ensure that you use the guidance correctly in your design and specifications and are able to justify any proposal that deviates from the recommendations. Do not rely on British Standards as if they are a specification in themselves.

British Standards that are pertinent to health, safety and well-being that you should be familiar with include:

- **BS 7974 Application of fire safety engineering principles to the design of buildings – Code of practice**. This standard sets out a framework for fire safety engineering principles in building design. The guidance provides recommendations and guidance for life safety and property and environmental protection with respect to fire safety, and covers both new and existing buildings.
- **BS 8560 Code of practice for the design of buildings incorporating safe work at height**. This standard sets out the considerations and issues of incorporating systems for safe work at height into the design of buildings. The guidance recommends early involvement by the design team and is aimed at designers and those involved in construction, inspection, cleaning and maintenance.
- **BS 9991 Fire safety in the design, management and use of residential buildings – Code of practice**. This standard provides recommendations and guidance for the design, management and use of residential buildings, focusing on ensuring the fire safety of all people. The standard applies to dwellings, residential accommodation blocks and specialised housing. Guidance covers designing means of escape, active fire protection, construction design, stairs and exits, HVAC, ancillary accommodation to flats and maisonettes, access and fire-fighting facilities, and building works.
- **BS 9999 Fire safety in the design, management and use of buildings – Code of practice**. This standard provides recommendations and guidance for the design, management and use of buildings, focusing on ensuring the fire safety of all people in and around buildings. The standard applies to new buildings and to alterations, extensions and changes of use of an existing building. Guidance covers the entire life cycle of a building, using a risk assessment approach and risk profiles, and looks at means of escape and evacuation strategy, access and fire-fighting facilities, building structure (including load and non-load bearing elements) and special risk protection.
- **BS EN 13501-1 Fire classification of construction products and building elements**. This standard provides a procedure for classifying

British Standards provide non-statutory guidance on ways to meet the functional requirements of the Building Regulations

**BS 9991:2015**
*Incorporating Corrigendum No.1*

BSI Standards Publication

**Fire safety in the design, management and use of residential buildings - Code of practice**

bsi.

all construction products[8] according to their reaction to fire considered in relation to their end use application[9]. Products can be classified, according to their fire performance, into seven ratings A1, A2, B, C, D, E and F, where A1 rated products are non-combustible and exhibit no sustained flaming when tested and F rated products are the most combustible, igniting within 20 seconds. A2, B, C, and D rated products may also be classified according to their propensity to produce smoke (s1, s2 or s3) and/or flaming droplets/particles (d0, d1 or d2) once ignited, where an s3 or d2 rating indicates the worst performance with unlimited production of smoke or flaming droplets/particles.

The Health and Safety Executive (HSE) publishes a wide range of non-statutory guidance documents relevant to many areas of health, safety and well-being, many of which are pertinent to the construction industry and our role as designers of the built environment.

Approved Codes of Practice (ACoPs), published by the HSE with the consent of the Secretary of State, provide practical advice and describe preferred or recommended methods that can be used (or standards to be met) to comply with regulations and the duties imposed by the HSWA. ACoPs have a special legal status. If you are prosecuted for breach of health and safety law, and it is proved that you did not follow the relevant provisions of an ACoP, you will need to show that you have complied with them in some other way or a court may find you at fault.[10]

Examples of HSE guidance that you should be familiar with include:

- **HSG168**: Fire safety in construction, which explains how everyone involved in a construction project can comply with their legal duties relating to fire risks.
- **L143**: Managing and working with asbestos, which provides guidance for employers about work which disturbs, or is likely to disturb, asbestos.
- **L153**: Managing health and safety in construction, which provides guidance on the legal requirements for the CDM Regulations, including the responsibilities of the duty holders under the regulations.

As part of your safety strategy, agree with your client and other members of the design team at the outset of your project which forms of non-statutory guidance you will follow to demonstrate compliance with any legislative requirements.

You may find that it may be necessary to use one piece of guidance to supplement another. For example, you might need to use BS 9991 to supplement the guidance in Approved Document B. However, do not pick and mix guidance from different sources, as it is essential that you adopt an integrated approach to your design.

Whilst non-statutory guidance is helpful in assisting you to understand your statutory duties, it is no substitute for taking the time to read and understand the statute itself. Likewise, you may find it helpful to seek advice from professional or legal advisers to help you navigate yourself around the various pieces of legislation. However, this always comes at the risk of advisers imposing an emphasis or bias on how to interpret or meet the intent of the legislation. To make sure you have a proper understanding of your statutory duties, always make time to read and digest the actual text of any legislation that is relevant to you, your clients and your projects.

## 5.3 Codes of conduct

**The ARB Code of Conduct** ('the ARB Code') sets out the minimum professional standards expected of all architects registered by the Architects Registration Board ('the ARB').

**'Standard 2 Competence'** of the ARB Code states that you are expected to be competent to carry out the professional work you undertake, and to keep your knowledge and skills relevant to your professional work up to date.

**'Standard 6 You should carry out your professional work conscientiously and with due regard to relevant technical and professional standards'** of

the ARB Code states that you are expected to carry out your work with skill and care.

**RIBA Code of Professional Conduct 2019** ('the Code') sets out and explains the standards of professional conduct and practice which the Royal Institute of British Architects ('the RIBA') requires of all its members. The Code applies to all members, whether they are working in traditional architectural practice or have followed a different career path, such as in a multidisciplinary organisation, academia or a construction company.

The purpose of the Code is to promote good conduct and best practice. Members must at all times comply with all relevant legal obligations but the Code does not seek to duplicate legal obligations.

**'Principal 2: Competence'** of the Code includes specific duties regarding the skill, knowledge, care and ability expected of all RIBA members.

If you are a member of the RIBA, your duties under the Code in connection with health and safety require you to:

- Be familiar and up to date with relevant codes of practice and guidelines which may be issued or endorsed by the RIBA from time to time, especially those concerned with health and safety, ethical practice, sustainability and protection of the environment (Principle 1.15).
- Have reasonable knowledge of, and abide by, all laws and regulations relating to health and safety as they apply to the design, construction and use of your building projects (Principle 6.1).
- Take reasonable steps[11] to ensure that your clients, and those with whom you have a direct professional relationship, are aware of and understand their responsibilities under the laws and regulations described in 6.1 above (Principle 6.2).
- Take reasonable steps to protect the health and safety of those under your direct control of instruction (Principle 6.3).

- Take reasonable steps to protect the health and safety of those carrying out, or likely to be directly affected by, construction work for which you are providing professional services. This includes clients and members of the public (Principle 6.4).
- Not enter into any contract which compromises your duty to protect health and safety (Principle 6.5).
- Notify your client if you become aware of anything which compromises or may compromise your duty to protect health and safety (Principle 6.6).
- Take appropriate action if you become aware of a decision taken by your employer or client which violates any law or regulation and that will, in your professional judgement, materially and adversely affect health and safety. This includes advising your employer or client against the decision, and/or refusing to consent to the decision, and/or reporting the decision to the local building inspector or other public official charged with the enforcement of the applicable laws and regulations, unless you are able to satisfactorily resolve the matter by other means (Principle 6.7).

# CHAPTER 6:
# CONSTRUCTION (DESIGN AND MANAGEMENT) REGULATIONS 2015

As soon as you carry out design in connection with any construction project based in Great Britain, including projects for a domestic client,[1] you assume legal duties under the Construction (Design and Management) Regulations 2015 ('the CDM Regulations'). The CDM Regulations apply to all construction projects as a whole – i.e. from concept to completion – and there is no minimum or maximum threshold in terms of size, type or value at which the CDM Regulations apply.

In this chapter we consider the legal duties imposed on designers and principal designers under the CDM Regulations:

6.1   Regulation 8 – General duties
6.2   Regulation 9 – Designer duties
6.3   Regulation 11 – Principal designer duties

Clients, principal contractors, contractors and workers also have duties under the CDM Regulations, but consideration of these, other than how they relate directly to designers and principal designers, is beyond the scope of this guidance.[2]

## 6.1 Regulation 8 – General Duties

You have general duties under Regulation 8, which apply to everyone working on a construction project.

The CDM Regulations impose different obligations on us as individual designers and on our practices as organisations. If you are employed in practice, a sole trader or self-employed, the obligations on a designer are most relevant. If you are the owner, partner or director of a practice, both the obligations of a designer and an organisation are relevant. Either way, it is important to understand the general duties of both to ensure they are being discharged appropriately on your project.

As a designer, you must have the appropriate skills, knowledge and experience to address the anticipated risks on your project and to complete the services you have been appointed to provide. You will need to determine for yourself, and demonstrate to your client, your relevant skills, knowledge and experience based on the complexity of each project on which you work. This should be done in a way that is specific and proportionate to the nature of each project, avoiding excessive or duplicated paperwork. One way to achieve this is to produce a CV that that is tailored to your client's current project and provides relevant details of your qualifications, professional memberships and experience of working on projects of a similar nature, size and complexity.

As a practice, you must have the organisational capability to perform the role and undertake the tasks for which your practice has been appointed. You need to demonstrate to your client that you have policies and systems in place to set acceptable health and safety standards within your practice, as well as the resources and people to deliver these at project level.

You need to be able to demonstrate as a minimum:

- how your practice manages building safety training and continuing professional development to ensure your designers' competence
- your system for design risk management and your review process to confirm that the system is being implemented effectively at project level
- your review process for checking building safety is being considered as part of your design development
- how you manage and ensure effective internal and external design team communication and cooperation.

Unless or until you have the appropriate skills, knowledge and experience, or your practice has the organisational capability, you must not accept or proceed with an appointment on a project.

Other general duties under Regulation 8 include the duty to:

- cooperate with anyone working in connection with your project (including people working on adjoining construction sites)
- report dangerous conditions

- provide clear, concise information or instructions in simple, comprehensible English and/or other languages where appropriate.

## 6.2. Regulation 9 – Designer duties

In addition to the general duties under Regulation 8, Regulation 9 sets out the duties that relate to all designers working on construction projects in Great Britain, including designers working overseas. These duties apply to all projects and at all stages, including concept designs, feasibility studies and competitions or speculative work.

You are deemed to be a designer under the CDM Regulations if you prepare or modify a design, or arrange or instruct someone under your control to do so.[3] These duties apply regardless of the status or nature of your appointment or any agreement you have with your client, including design work you may carry out for no fee or for a friend or family member.

Design work includes drawings, design details, specifications and bills of quantities (including specification of articles or substances) relating to a structure, and includes calculations prepared for the purpose of a design.

As well as being aware of your duties as a designer, before you commence any design work on your project you have a duty to satisfy yourself that your client is aware of their duties under the CDM Regulations. To do this you need to be sufficiently aware of the client's duties, which are set out in Regulations 4 to 6 and include:

- Duties in relation to managing the project, including making sure enough time and sufficient resources are available for the duration of the project, to ensure that the construction work can be carried out, so far as is reasonably practicable, without risks to the health or safety of any person affected by the project; and that welfare facilities are provided for those carrying out construction work. (Regulation 4).
- A duty to appoint a principal designer and a principal contractor, where it is reasonably foreseeable that more than one contractor will be working on the project at any one time. If your client fails to make

either or both appointments, the client must fulfil the role or roles (Regulation 5).
- Notifying the HSE about the project prior to construction starting on site, by submitting an F10 form if construction work is scheduled to last longer than 30 working days and has more than 20 workers working simultaneously, or exceeds 500 person days (Regulation 6).
- Ensuring that you comply with your designer duties, including if you are working outside Great Britain (Regulation 10).

Regulation 7 deals specifically with the duties of domestic clients, which delegates the client duties to the principal contractor. If you have a domestic client and they fail to make these appointments, the designer in control of the pre-construction phase of the project is the principal designer (Regulation 7(2)(a)) and the contractor in control of the construction phase of the project is the principal contractor (Regulation 7(2)(b)).

Use your client briefing process to assess your client's level of knowledge and experience of the CDM Regulations to decide the appropriate detail and format for the advice you need to give them regarding their duties. Do not wait until you have been formally appointed to do this because it may be too late, particularly if you are involved at the bid or feasibility stage of the project. If a principal designer has been appointed, request written confirmation that the client has been adequately advised of their duties to ensure your obligation as a designer is met.

Discuss design risk management with your client at the outset of your project. The greatest opportunities for positive influence on the safety of your project without design compromise are at the concept and pre-planning design stages of the project. The strategic decisions you make with your client regarding height, massing and spatial arrangements directly impact on how safely your project can be constructed, occupied and maintained. The design, quality and safety of your project may be undermined if residual risks you failed to design-out at the early design stages have to be controlled and managed by employing safety systems that may result in a greater likelihood of accidents.

When you prepare your design – or modify a design prepared by others – you have a duty to consider the general principles of prevention and any pre-construction information provided by your client to eliminate, so far as reasonably practicable, foreseeable risks to the health and safety of any person. This includes anyone involved in the construction, maintenance or occupation of your project.

If you are unable to eliminate any risks, after you have taken steps to reduce their impact through your design, you have a duty to provide your client's principal designer with clear, concise information regarding these residual risks. This may be in the form of a residual risk register, annotations or safety symbols on your model or drawings, or schedules on drawings (sometimes referred to as Safety, Health and Environment boxes, or SHE boxes).

If you have designed-out all unusual or significant risks from your project, let the principal designer know, so that everyone is aware that no unusual risks or special measures are required in connection with the architectural elements of the project.

In addition to residual risk information, you have a duty to provide information about the design, construction and maintenance of the architectural aspects of your project. This will assist your client, all other designers and any contractors to comply with their duties under the CDM Regulations.

## 6.3 Regulation 11 – Principal designer duties

If it is reasonably foreseeable that more than one contractor at a time will be working on your project, your client has a duty under the CDM Regulations to appoint a designer to be the principal designer with control over health and safety in the pre-construction phase of the project.

The principal designer's appointment must be in writing and made as soon as practicable before the construction phase begins, ideally at the concept design stage. If your client fails to appoint a principal designer, they must fulfil the principal designer's duties. If your client is a domestic client, the designer in control of the pre-construction phase will be the principal designer.

If you are appointed as principal designer, make sure your principal designer appointment is separate from your designer appointment, including a separate fee and schedule of services. Your duties as a principal designer are separate and distinct from your duties as a designer and you need to have sufficient dedicated resources in place to provide the principal designer services appropriately.

Your principal designer appointment should be in place for as long as you are working for your client and there is a need for pre-construction design services. Bear in mind that the pre-construction design work for some elements of work may run simultaneously with work that has already reached the construction phase. Accordingly, your appointment and principal designer duties will continue during the construction phase.

The principal designer must be a direct appointment with your client. If you are working on a design and build project and your design appointment is novated to the contractor, your principal designer appointment with your client will need to be terminated to avoid any post-novation conflicts of interest. In this case, your client will need to appoint a new principal designer, who may be the principal contractor, to replace you and to manage any remaining pre-construction information.

In addition to the general duties under Regulation 8, Regulation 11 sets out the duties of a principal designer. Your primary duty as a principal designer is to plan, manage and monitor the pre-construction phase to ensure that, so far as is reasonably practicable, the project is carried out without risks to health and safety.

The pre-construction phase covers any phase of your project during which design work is being carried out and may continue during the construction phase.

Whilst your duties as a principal designer do not include any specific design duties (these fall under your appointment as a designer), you still need to apply the principles of prevention and to identify, eliminate and control, as far as is reasonably practicable, foreseeable risks to anyone involved in the construction, occupation and maintenance of your project. This requires you to consider all available information when decisions are being taken regarding the planning and sequencing or phasing of design and construction work, including estimating the time and resources required to complete the work.

The information likely to be available to you includes pre-construction information provided by your client, any construction phase plans that have been produced by the principal contractor and are relevant to design taking place during the construction phase, and any existing health and safety file provided in relation to the existing construction of your project.

Whilst your client is responsible for providing you with any pre-construction information that is already in their possession, as principal designer you will need to assist the client to collate this information, assess its adequacy, identify any gaps and advise the client regarding what additional information may be required. You are then responsible for ensuring the pre-construction information is provided in a convenient form to any designers and contractors working on your project – or being considered – to enable them to carry out their duties.

To fulfil your principal designer duties, you need to ensure that, so far as is reasonably practicable, all other designers working on your project comply with their duties under Regulation 9 and that everyone working on the pre-construction phase cooperates with your client, with you and with each other.

The most effective way to achieve this is to implement early, regular and effective communication between all the other designers working on your project (including specialists and contractors with design responsibility). The best way to do this is to ensure design risk management is incorporated into all regular design workshops or design team meetings and in progress meetings with the client and principal contractor. Use these regular meetings to discuss design risks, agree control measures required for risks that cannot be eliminated and agree the format and content of pre-construction information that the principal contractor will require to prepare the construction phase plan.

As the principal designer, you are not expected to be a health and safety expert or adviser[4] and you are not responsible for the other designers' designs or for advising the other designers on how they should eliminate risks or modify their design. This remains each designer's responsibility under the CDM Regulations. You are responsible for ensuring that the other designers identify the foreseeable risks in their design and coordinate this information to ensure clear, concise and relevant project specific information regarding significant and unusual residual risks is communicated to the client and principal contractor. Promptly alert your client if you have any concerns regarding a designer's competence, ability or willingness to carry out their duties appropriately.

Regulation 12 sets out the principal designer's duties with respect to the construction phase plan and health and safety file.

As principal designer, you must assist the principal contractor in preparing the construction phase plan for your project by providing the principal contractor with a copy of all the relevant pre-construction information you have obtained from the client, and the relevant design and residual risk information you have obtained from the other designers.

During the pre-construction phase, and for the duration of your appointment as principal designer, you are responsible for compiling the health and safety file, commencing work on this at the outset of your project. Subsequently, regularly review and update it to take account of the progress of the works and any changes to the design and construction. Even if you know your appointment as principal designer will be terminated prior to commencement of the construction phase, you should prepare a health and safety file with the relevant pre-construction and designers' information available to you before your appointment is terminated.

The health and safety file should only include project specific information that is clear, concise and likely to be relevant to ensuring the safety of anyone planning, or carrying out, future maintenance or construction work on your project. Do not include generic information, risk assessments, information regarding obvious hazards or risks that have been eliminated during the pre-construction or construction phases.

If you are appointed as principal designer for the duration of the construction phase of your project, pass the completed health and safety file to your client at the end of the project. If your appointment is terminated prior to completion of your project, pass the health and safety file to the principal contractor. They will assume responsibility for completing it and passing it on to the client when the project completes.

As principal designer, you are not responsible for ensuring the competency of the other designers, the principal contractor or the other contractors; this is your client's responsibility. The only exception is if you are appointing a designer as a sub-consultant. In this case you become their client and assume the client duties with respect to ensuring they have the relevant skills, knowledge and expertise to fulfil their designer duties.

You are also not responsible for providing health and safety advice to your client or the project team, other than in respect of their duties under the CDM Regulations. If you, your client or any members of the design and construction team require specialist health and safety advice, recommend that your client appoints a health and safety adviser.

If you do not have the skills, knowledge and expertise to provide principal designer services, one way to develop this experience is to appoint a health and safety adviser as your sub-consultant to provide you with the relevant advice to enable you to discharge your duties. Be aware, however, that you cannot delegate your statutory obligations under the CDM Regulations to a sub-consultant and that you remain liable under the regulations for discharging your duties correctly.

# CHAPTER 7:
# PRINCIPLES OF FIRE SAFETY DESIGN

To ensure our design risk management with respect to fire safety design is effective, we need to understand some of the basic principles of fire science and how construction materials perform in the event of a fire.

In this chapter, we consider the aspects of fire and fire safety design with which you need to be familiar:

7.1   Ignition, development and spread of fire
7.2   Fire performance of construction materials
7.3   Design for fire safety

The guidance in this chapter provides a base from which fire safety can be included in the design risk management process. When appropriate, you should seek advice from a suitably qualified and competent fire safety specialist.

# 7.1 IGNITION, DEVELOPMENT AND SPREAD OF FIRE

**Ignition** of a fire requires an exothermic chemical chain reaction to take place that combines a source of heat, fuel and oxygen. As long as all three of these elements are present, this chemical reaction will sustain a fire. Eliminating one of these elements will extinguish the fire (for example, cooling the seat of the fire, removing the source of fuel or excluding oxygen from the atmosphere of the fire). There are many causes of ignition but typical examples that affect construction sites and/ or construction projects include:

- electrical faults
- uncontrolled hot works
- discarded cigarettes that have not been properly extinguished
- arson.

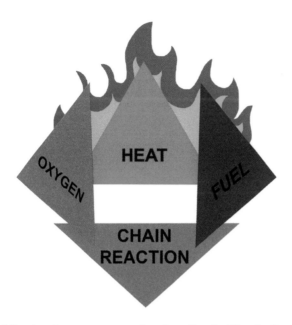

Components of an exothermic chemical chain reaction required to sustain fire

**Phases of fire development** are used to describe the life of a fire from its ignition to its decay. There are five distinct phases of fire development:

1. The **ignition/incipient phase**, when heat, fuel and oxygen combine in a sustained chemical reaction. This phase typically results in a small fire and this is when the possibility of extinguishing the fire is greatest.

2. The **growth phase**, when the fire develops as heat from the incipient fire spreads to adjacent combustible materials that act as additional fuel sources and ignite. At this stage, active fire suppression measures – such as sprinklers or mist systems – may extinguish the fire or limit its further growth.

3. The **flashover phase**, when combustible materials within the space containing the fire ignite simultaneously. This normally occurs at temperatures of **500°C or above.** Flashover occurs when heat radiating off a buoyant layer of hot smoke, which has spread across the ceiling of a confined room, causes combustible materials in the room to thermally decompose, releasing flammable gases that then ignite.

Phases of fire
development and decay

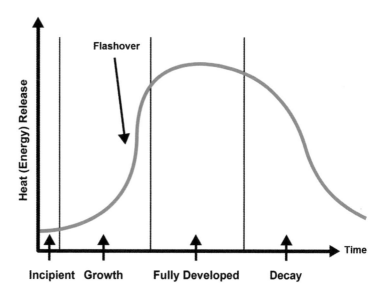

4. The **fully developed phase**, when the growth phase reaches its peak. The temperature of the fire is at its highest and all combustible materials will have been ignited, consuming all available fuel. During this phase, fire safety relies on containment or compartmentation by fire-resisting construction to prevent further fire spread.

5. The **decay phase**, also known as burnout, when there is a significant decrease in fuel and/or oxygen available to support continued combustion. This results in a fall in the temperature and intensity of the fire, eventually resulting in the fire being extinguished. During this phase, if oxygen is rapidly reintroduced to the oxygen depleted environment (for example, by someone opening a door to the room containing the fire), superheated gasses in the fire will rapidly and explosively burn, creating a backdraft.

**Fire spread** can occur in three different ways as heat energy from a fire is transferred to adjacent combustible materials, raising their temperature to the point of ignition. These are:

1. **Convection**, which occurs in fluids and gases when heat transferred from the fire causes the fluid or gas to heat and become less dense

and rise, spreading heat away from the vicinity of the fire (for example, when air heated by the fire rises and spreads across the ceiling of a room).

2. **Conduction**, which occurs when heat from the fire is transferred between two materials that are in direct contact with each other (for example, when heat is transferred across a solid wall from the side facing on to a fire to the side facing away from the fire).

3. **Radiation**, which occurs when heat from the fire is transferred by electromagnetic waves (for example, the heat you feel being emitted from an electric fire). Radiant heat from a fire can preheat fuels ahead of the fire, increasing the likelihood, speed and intensity of the growth phase.

Methods of heat transfer that can lead to fire spread

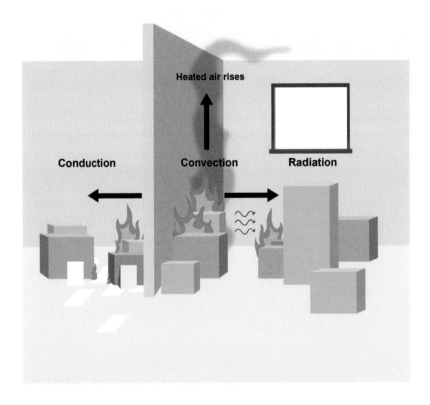

## 7.2 FIRE PERFORMANCE OF CONSTRUCTION MATERIALS

The fire performance of construction materials can be classified by two different characteristics:

1.  a material's reaction to fire
2.  its fire resistance.

**Reaction to fire** is the measure of whether and to what degree a material, product or system will contribute to fire spread. This is done by determining how combustible a material is, how much smoke it will produce once ignited and whether any pieces of the material will sustain combustion.

A material's reaction to fire can be tested, assessed and classified in accordance with BS EN 13501-1. These test results provide a classification from A1 (highest performance i.e. non-combustible) to F (lowest performance). Untested materials cannot be classified.[1]

The classification of a material tested to BS EN 13501-1 will be identified by assessing its gross calorific potential in megajoules per kilogram, temperature rise, mass loss, fire growth rate and duration of sustained flaming.

Combustible materials, products and systems (those rated A2, B, C, D and E) can also be assessed and classified in accordance with BS EN 13501-1 to determine their potential to produce smoke or create flaming droplets. The sub-classifications for smoke production are: s1, s2 or s3, with s1 indicating the lowest production and s3 indicating no limit on smoke production.

Flaming droplets are small particles or pieces of material that, after separating from the source material, continue to burn for a period of time and therefore risk contributing to the spread of fire. The sub-classifications for flaming droplets are: d0, d1 or d2, with d0 indicating no production and d2 indicating no limitation of the production of flaming droplets.

Materials classified as meeting A1 produce very limited smoke and no flaming droplets.

**Fire resistance** is the ability of a material, component or system to satisfy, for a stated period of time, some or all of the criteria given in a relevant test standard. Fire resistance is measured in minutes, which describes the time elapsed in a standard test rather than real time.

Fire resistance is a measure of one or more of the following:

- Resistance to collapse – a loadbearing element's *loadbearing capacity*. This is denoted **R** in the European classification of the resistance to fire performance.
- Resistance to fire penetration – a measure of a product's *integrity*. This is denoted **E** in the European classification of the resistance to fire performance.
- Resistance to the transfer of excessive heat – a measure of a product's capacity to perform as *insulation*. This is denoted **I** in the European classification of the resistance to fire performance.

Different elements of construction may have combinations of R, E and I. For example, a structural member such as a beam or a column will only have a loadbearing capacity (R), a loadbearing compartment wall or floor will have a loadbearing capacity, integrity and insulation (R, E and I), while a non-loadbearing element such as a partition or a door will only have integrity and insulation (E and I).

The periods of fire resistance given in technical guidance are based on assumptions about the severity of a potential fire and the consequences of any element of a structure failing. Fire severity is estimated in very broad terms based on buildings' uses (their purpose group) and on the assumption that buildings' contents (which constitute the fire load) are similar for buildings in the same purpose group.

Several factors affect the specified period(s) of fire resistance that you will need to specify when designing your project. These include:

- The amount of combustible material per unit of floor area for the type of building you are designing. This is known as the fire load density.
- The height of the top floor of your proposed building above the lowest external ground level. This impacts on evacuation, firefighting and the potential consequences of structural failure.
- The occupancy type, which will determine how quickly and easily your building can be evacuated.
- Whether your project includes any basements. The limited external elevational area of basements limits opportunities for ventilation and access in the event of a fire. This in turn can increase the heat build-up, fire spread and duration of a fire, as well as causing problems for firefighting.
- Whether your building is a single storey and therefore is easy to evacuate and a low risk of structural failure.

**Testing and certification** is critical in helping you to understand the reaction to fire and fire resistance of any material, product or system you propose to specify, including any limitations on their use.

Appropriate testing information that you should obtain from the manufacturer or supplier prior to specifying a material, product or system should include **third-party certification** produced following an independent test and assessment by an UKAS[2] accredited testing and certification body. This will provide you with confirmation that the manufacturer's declaration of the fire performance of the materials, product or system have been met under test conditions.

Where it is not possible to obtain third-party certification, an assessment or technical evaluation produced by an accredited fire test laboratory or qualified fire consultant may be used. This will provide you with an expert judgement regarding a material, product or system in lieu of third-party certification.[3] This may be necessary if the size or use of the material, product or system make it impractical to use a standard test method.

Designers can request a fire test report documenting the results of the British or European Standard fire test that has been carried out by a manufacturer for the material, product or system that you intend to specify. This will provide you with a report that is specific to the fire performance of the specific material, product or system that has been tested, including its finish and colour. You should not rely on indicative or ad-hoc tests that have not been carried out in accordance with a British or European Standard fire test; nor should you rely on a test report for a similar product.

Any test evidence you use to determine or demonstrate the fire performance of a material, product or system you intend to specify must be checked to ensure that it is applicable to your intended use. Small differences in detail – such as fixing method, joints, dimensions, the introduction of insulation materials and air gaps (ventilated or not) – can significantly affect the fire performance of a material, product or system.

When you are selecting materials, products or systems for use in the construction of an external wall for a relevant building, you will need to demonstrate that they meet the functional requirements of Building Regulations Part B4.

There are three ways you can do this, which are referred to as routes to compliance:

1. Only specifying materials that have had their fire performance tested and certified with a European Class rating in accordance with BS EN 13501-1 appropriate for their intended use.
2. Procuring an independent third-party, full-scale fire test to demonstrate that your proposed wall construction meets the performance criteria given in BRE 135 for external walls using full-scale test data from **BS 8414-1:2020** or **BS 8414-2:2020 Fire performance of external cladding systems**.
3. Where it is impractical or not feasible to carry out a full-scale test, procuring an assessment in lieu of a test in accordance with **BS EN 9414 – Fire performance of external cladding systems based on the application of test results in accordance with BS 8414-1 and**

**BS 8414-2 or BS EN 15725 – Extended application reports on the fire performance of construction products and building elements**. You should only rely on this form of assessment when sufficient and relevant test evidence is available to support the assessments, and the assessment has been prepared by an organisation with the necessary expertise (for example, an organisation listed as a notified body in accordance with the European Construction Products Regulations or a laboratory accredited by UKAS for the relevant test standard).

In England, the Building Regulations limit the use of combustible materials in the external walls and specified attachments of relevant buildings. Regulation 7 of the Building Regulations defines the scope of relevant buildings, the reaction to fire classification that materials in external walls must meet (European Class A1 or A2, s1, d0) and a list of materials that are exempt from the limitations.

## 7.3 DESIGN FOR FIRE SAFETY

**Passive and active fire protection** provide the first line of defence to preventing fire growth and spread. The effectiveness of the fire protection measures in a building will also impact on the success of the evacuation strategy and provisions for firefighting.

Passive fire protection refers to static systems that are part of a building's construction (for example, fire-resisting construction used to create fire compartments to contain fire spread). These systems do not require a command signal or intervention to operate.

Examples of passive fire protection include, but are not limited to:

- fire-rated walls and floors
- fire-rated door sets
- fire-rated ductwork and dampers
- cavity barriers, fire stops and fire collars
- alternative means of escape

- protected refuges
- fire-rated firefighting shafts, stairwells and lobbies.

Active fire protection refers to systems that require a command signal or positive action to activate them in the event of a fire. The action may be manual (for example, a portable fire extinguisher) or automatic (for example, a sprinkler system). Manual active systems are more likely to require regular maintenance and testing, and may require building owners/occupiers to be trained in their use and operation. Automatic active fire protection systems also need careful design and specification to ensure they have fail-safe mechanisms and back-up sources of power to confirm they are operational in the event of a fire.

Examples of active fire protection include, but are not limited to:

- smoke, heat and fire detection and alarm systems
- automatic fire suppression systems (for example, sprinkler, mist or $CO_2$ suppression systems)
- mechanical smoke ventilation systems (for example, automatic opening vents)
- dry and wet risers
- emergency communication systems
- portable fire extinguishers
- emergency lighting.

Passive and active fire protection systems address different aspects of fire protection and are co-dependent, often working together to provide an effective fire protection strategy. For example, fire-rated construction will prevent fire spread whilst an automatic suppression system will limit fire growth. You should consider how this combination – or layers of fire protection – can be used most effectively in the design of your project to produce a comprehensive fire safety strategy that complements your client's requirements for the use, operation and maintenance of the project. As part of your design risk management you should consider the potential impact on your fire strategy of one or more layers of fire protection failing, particularly if you are relying on several active fire protection systems.

**Evacuation strategies** and the role they play should be a fundamental part of your fire safety strategy and an intrinsic part of the design development of your project.

The evacuation strategy that you adopt will impact on the design choices you make with respect to:

- travel distances
- dead end corridors or single means of escape
- the clear widths of escape routes
- passive and active fire protection measures
- access for firefighting.

When occupants are alerted to fire in a building, they have to make a series of decisions before evacuating. Different people will respond in different ways. The major influence on what they think and do is the nature of the organisational or social unit of which they are a part rather than the design of the building. This broadly relates to the type of building in which occupants experience the emergency. For example, are they familiar with their surroundings at home or work or are they in a building where they are unfamiliar with the layout? Further guidance regarding the principles of human behaviour during an emergency is provided in the Appendix.

Understanding human behaviour and responses to a fire, as well as the impact of design on means of warning and evacuation, can inform your design decisions but you should always balance this with your responsibility to meet your statutory duties and to comply with relevant fire safety design guidance.

The evacuation strategy that is most appropriate for your project will generally depend on its use, size and provision for firefighting. The evacuation strategies that you should consider are:

- **Delayed evacuation**. This includes a remain in place or stay put strategy, which is common in residential developments. This strategy involves limited evacuation of those at direct risk from the fire whilst the majority of occupants remain in the building as the fire is tackled by the fire service. This strategy relies on adequate fire and smoke compartmentation and requires a suitable alternative evacuation plan in case a full evacuation becomes necessary.

- **Phase evacuation.** This strategy is used for buildings where it is not desirable or practical to evacuate all the occupants simultaneously, but delayed evacuation and a stay put strategy is not appropriate (for example, in care homes where the residents require additional time and assistance to prepare for and undertake evacuation). When this approach is used for high-rise residential buildings, the residents most at risk from a fire are evacuated first, including any residents requiring assistance as described in a Personal Emergency Evacuation Plan (see below). Remaining residents are then evacuated in phases, usually two storeys at a time.

- **Progressive evacuation**. This strategy is used when it is not possible for occupants to evacuate the building simultaneously. The strategy involves moving occupants to temporary places of safety within the building where they can remain until they can be evacuated safely. There are two managed strategies:
  1. **Progressive horizontal evacuation**, which involves moving people to an adjoining fire compartment on the same building level. This is a common strategy used in hospitals.
  2. **Zoned evacuation**, which involves moving people away from an affected zone to an adjacent zone. This is a common strategy used in large retail developments.

- **Simultaneous evacuation**. This strategy is adopted when the effects of a fire render it unsafe for occupants to remain in the building. This strategy can be executed in two ways:
  1. **Single-staged evacuation**, which is instigated by a building-wide instantaneous evacuation signal from the fire detection and alarm system.
  2. **Two-staged or double-knock evacuation**, which allows for an investigation period prompted by a localised fire detection and alarm before building-wide evacuation fire alarm systems are activated.

- A **Personal Emergency Evacuation Plan (PEEP)** is a bespoke evacuation strategy for an individual who may not be able to reach an ultimate place of safety unaided or within a satisfactory period of time in the event of any emergency. A **Generic Emergency Evacuation Plan (GEEP)** provides a similar form of evacuation strategy for a visitor to a building who may require assistance to evacuate the building.

**Provision for firefighting** is a function requirement of the Building Regulations in England, in accordance with Part B5 Access and facilities for the fire service. It includes a requirement to provide reasonable facilities to assist firefighters, as well as reasonable provision to enable firefighters to gain access to your building.

You should consider the aspects of your design that will impact on access and facilities for the fire service from RIBA Work Stage 2 Concept Design, as part of your fire safety strategy. Guidance regarding appropriate ways to achieve this and how to meet the functional requirements of the Building Regulations is provided in Approved Document B and the British and European standards we considered in Chapter 5.

Understanding the principles of firefighting operations will assist you in developing an appropriate fire safety strategy for your project with your client and their project team. This will be dependent on the nature of your project – the building type and use, its location and size, its occupancy characteristics and your proposed evacuation strategy. The passive and active fire protection measures that you incorporate into your design to ensure the safety of occupants and safe evacuation will also ensure the safety of firefighters. Fire protection measures such as compartmentation, smoke ventilation/extraction and fire suppression systems will provide firefighters with sufficient time to fight a fire.

Additional measures that you should consider incorporating into your building to assist firefighters include providing:

- appropriate vehicular access for firefighting appliances
- fire mains and hydrants
- firefighting shafts (including stairs and lifts)
- basement ventilation.

A detailed commentary regarding these measures is beyond the scope of this guidance. However, if you work on multi-storey and/or multiple-occupancy buildings or structures you should be aware of how your design may impact on firefighting operations.

Firefighting operations involving multi-storey buildings are usually conducted from within the building. The use of external firefighting operations tends to be limited to when fire protection measures have failed, fire spread is out of control and there is a need to contain the fire to prevent it spreading to neighbouring buildings.

This means the vertical circulation core(s) in the building must be designed to fulfil two important and separate functions:

1. Provide a safe smoke-free route out of the building for occupants.
2. Provide a safe route to and from the bridgehead (see below) for firefighters to fight the fire and carry out effective search and rescue operations.

A conflict can arise when these functions must take place at the same time, particularly in single-staircase buildings. Firefighters, often with bulky breathing apparatus, ascending a staircase to reach a fire will hinder the use of the staircase for evacuation. Once the firefighters connect their branch hose(s) to a charged dry riser at the bridgehead, they will need to run the hose(s) from the bridgehead up to the incident floor via the staircase, potentially blocking access for evacuation. Fire doors on the incident floor will then be held open by the charged hose(s) which can result in the staircase filling with smoke, further compromising access for evacuation.

Firefighting in multi-storey buildings is typically deployed over several storeys and managed using a 'vertical sectorisation model'. This model is used by firefighters to describe and organise a building into areas of firefighting activity, known as sectors. This sectorisation enables firefighters to manage and control firefighting operations more effectively, particularly when sector commanders cannot be physical present in the

Access to a staircase can be compromised by fire-fighters and charged hosepipes between the bridgehead and incident floor of a building

sector, due to smoke or heat for example. These sectors are identified as follows:

Vertical sectorisation model

- The **bridgehead**, which is normally located at least two storeys below the fire floor, provided that these storeys are clear of smoke, and is the main command point from which firefighting and search and rescue operations are managed on site. To avoid overwhelming the bridgehead with firefighting personnel, a staging area one storey below the bridgehead may be required as a holding area for firefighters awaiting instructions. The bridgehead and staging area refer to locations in the building rather than a sector.
- The **fire sector** is an operational sector and is the main zone of firefighting and rescue operations. The fire sector comprises the storeys from the bridgehead, the fire floor(s) directly involved in the fire – known as the incident floor(s) – and one storey above.
- The **search sector** is an operational sector that is located above the fire sector where search and rescue and ventilation are taking place.
- The **lobby sector** is a support sector and covers the area of operations from the ground floor lobby to the bridgehead.

The vertical sectorisation model illustrated depends on effective compartmentation within a building to contain fire spread. If a compartment fails and fire spreads horizontally or vertically beyond its original compartment, identifying and managing the sectors becomes dynamic and more difficult. This may also result in a change in the firefighting and/or evacuation strategy (for example, moving from a delayed strategy to a simultaneous strategy).

The guidance on fire safety in this chapter has been produced to bridge the gap between technical guidance with which designers will be familiar – including Approved Documents and British Standards – and the principles that underpin fire safety in buildings. Designers should exercise reasonable skill, care and diligence in the performance of their services and should identify when further expertise, in the form of a fire safety specialist, is required.

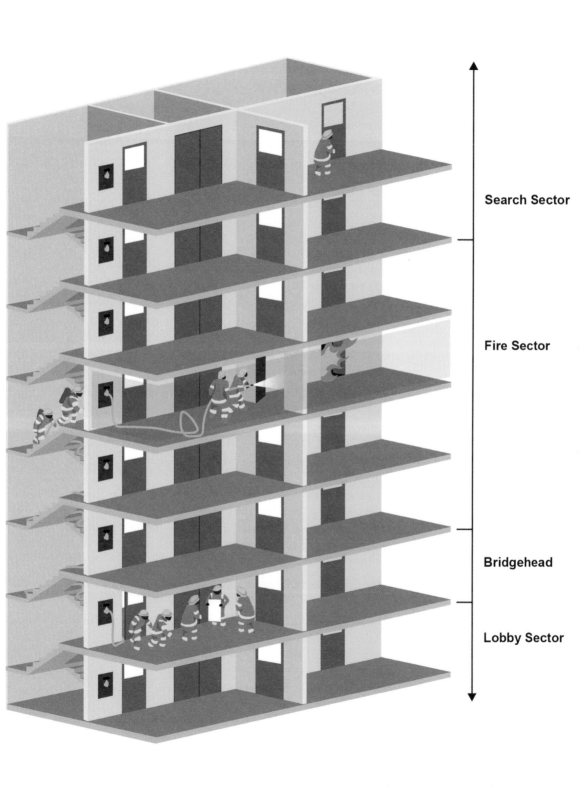

# AFTERWORD

Why does all this matter?

Because, 72 people lost their lives in the early hours of 14 June 2017, more than 70 people were injured and countless more had their lives changed forever when a domestic fire at Grenfell Tower, west London, burnt out of control, resulting in the most catastrophic residential fire in the UK since the Second World War.

We may not know all the precise details of the circumstances that led to the events on that fateful night, but what we do know is that as a profession we played our part by failing to act on the lessons learnt from a similar fire at Lakanal House, south London, in 2009.

Dame Judith Hackitt's review of the building regulatory system, 'Building a Safer Future', has identified a need for systemic change in behaviours and attitudes to safety in the construction industry. Hackitt has made 52 recommendations for change, all of which have been supported by government. Many of these recommendations will require us to change our approach and attitude to how we deliver our services as designers, principal designers and lead designers.

As a profession, and more importantly as individuals, it is our duty to ensure we embrace this change, to take proper responsibility for the design work we undertake and to remind ourselves of the important role we play in shaping the built environment.

This has to start by ensuring that every one of us is competent to fulfil the responsibilities entrusted to us to design buildings that are safe. This includes a responsibility to do everything we can to play our part in improving the construction industry and to collaborate with others to deliver buildings that are safe, both now and in the future.

We owe it to everyone whose life has been impacted by the Grenfell Tower fire to do everything we can to see that such a disaster never happens again.

Dieter Bentley-Gockmann
EPR Architects
June 2020

# APPENDIX I: PRINCIPLES OF HUMAN BEHAVIOUR DURING AN EMERGENCY

## Warning and Escape in Case of Fire

Our interventions are not only shaped by their context, purpose and construction methodology, but also by overarching legislative requirements. In the event of a fire, the regulations specifically set out several requirements, one of which is the need to provide the appropriate provision for communicating or warning of fire, and the appropriate means of escape in case of fire.

There are several approaches that can be followed in order to demonstrate compliance with this regulatory requirement, for example, using approved document guidance or the application of fire safety engineering principles. These approaches provide guidance based on the time taken for an individual to move from their initial position to a place of safety in an emergency. The time taken is generally expressed as a travel distance to enable a designer to set out an escape route. Calculations and modelling using computational tools, and qualitative design review can also be used to benchmark designs against regulations and other requirements and recommendations.

These routes to compliance do not account for the actual actions of individuals before and during a fire, which can delay their exit. There are however several models that begin to address behaviours performed by occupants during fires, such as EXODUS which focusses on five core interacting sub-models – occupant, movement, behaviour, Toxicity and Hazards, and CRISP (Comparison of Risk Indices by Simulation Procedures), a risk assessment model which focusses on the physical and chemical process of fire in relation to the behaviours of occupants attempting to escape or suppress the fire.

## Human Behaviour in an Emergency

In order to recognise the impact of human behaviours in fire, and the effect of active and passive layers of fire protection, we need to understand and appreciate how these two fundamental aspects directly impact occupant safety. Human behaviour specifically focuses upon patterns and actions developed through an individual's decision-making process, dependent on the type of building, and design related to aid an occupant's safety should they decide to, or need to, stay put or leave.

Understanding human behavioural patterns and response in a fire or other emergencies, as well as the impact of design on means of warning and escape, can begin to inform design decisions, but should not unfavourably impact upon your responsibilities to meet baseline legislative requirements (See Chapter 5 – Statute, Guidance and Codes of Conduct).

When alerted to a fire in a building the users have to make a series of decisions. Although different people may respond in different ways, the major influence on what they think and do is not the design details, but the nature of the organisational or social unit they are part of. This broadly relates to the type of building in which they experience the emergency.

## Decision-making in an emergency

This model identifies the process of decision-making in an emergency, such as a fire, through several stages and highlights various routes that illustrate behaviour patterns between three distinct stages:

**STAGE**

Model of Human
Behaviour in an
emergency[1]

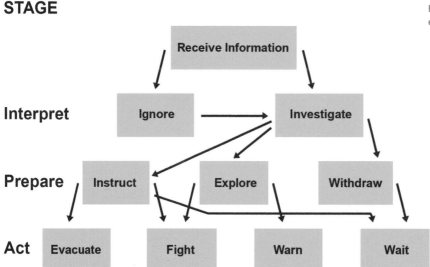

- **Interpret:** The process is triggered when an individual is presented with initial cues ('receiving information'), upon which there is a decision to investigate further ('investigate') or misinterprets these initial cues ('ignore').
- **Prepare:** Once a fire has been identified, the individual will attempt to seek further information (explore), inform others ('instruct') or remove themselves from the situation ('withdraw').
- **Act:** The final stage, the individual will deal with the fire ('fight'), interact with others ('warn') and either leave ('evacuate') or stay ('wait').

This model can be used to describe the decision process during a fire, where the organisational structure of different building types creates a set of social rules that inform a pattern of occupant's decisions when seeking information and taking action during a fire. Using different building types, the following examples show how the decisions made when interpreting, preparing and acting, during a fire, relates to organisational and social structures.

The final stage of acting can be hindered through the design of buildings. A typical plan which is repetitious across the number of stories of a building, or simple plan where it is easy to orientate yourself, such as sightlines to escape routes (stairs and lifts), avoids confusion to occupants trying to leave. In complex layouts where the plan form changes between storeys, this can cause poor awareness of access and escape routes requiring careful wayfinding in the design. Typically, if occupants can find their way around building under normal conditions then they will be able to in an emergency.

## Human Behaviours in Different Building Types and Organisational Structures

### Homes

Occupants generally misinterpret or ignore cues of a fire and will only investigate further where cues persist. Each occupant tends to investigate the situation themselves to confirm the presence of a fire, even if confirmed by other occupants. Before evacuating, there may be some attempt to fight the fire, which is particularly characteristic of domestic fires as opposed to other building types.

### Multioccupancy Residential

Occupants often receive ambiguous cues which are likely to be followed by a process of misinterpretations. Occupants may find it confusing and difficult to understand if they are the prime discoverer of a fire, or one of many individuals with a similar experience. During evacuation, most individuals return to their flat before evacuating the building, and their awareness of the likelihood of meeting others is demonstrated by their actions of dressing and gathering valuables, delaying their exit.

### Hotels

Similar to multioccupancy residential buildings, guests receive, misinterpret and investigate the cues of a fire. Invariably, guests would inform a member of staff, and seek information from an authoritative source in preparation to act. This influences the actions of the guests, where instructions are relayed from hotel staff, primarily from guests telephoning the hotel reception. Dressing, gathering valuables and packing are common in these emergency situations, and guests would usually evacuate by the available stairs, even if hindered by smoke.

### Offices

In offices, occupants are usually familiar with their surroundings (including various escape routes from frequent fire safety drills) and have a clearer knowledge of their organisational structure and hierarchy. The process of decision-making is directed around the organisational structure, and although occupants will investigate cues and may confirm the effects of a fire, or potential fire, they will alert senior members of staff rather than explore further.

### Public Buildings

In public buildings, there is a reliance on people in authority (usually staff) for information. Many people in the early stages of fire growth will tend to continue to carry out ineffective actions, most notably delaying their own response to the early warnings. Staff may investigate and try to address the fire themselves, even when they acknowledge that helping people to evacuate the building is the most effective option. Usually, when appropriate information is provided to the public, evacuation is frequently rapid.

### Hospitals

Detection and investigation of a fire takes place relatively early when compared with other occupancies. This is due to the more general spread of people throughout the building and the fact that there is always somebody awake, on duty. Routes of escape are carefully pre-planned and during a fire they are relayed by senior staff and assisted by junior staff, removing decision-making from patients and visitors.

# Key patterns of human behaviour

Research findings since the early 1990s have highlighted a series of familiar behavioural patterns and actions of occupants during a fire. In most cases, occupants continue to act in a way that they know is appropriate, for example, leave the way they came in. These propositions not only take account for the objective physical environment, but people's knowledge of a building layout and information available about a fire threat.

- In the early stages of an emergency, occupants seek to obtain clear information and/or direction from an authoritative figure to tell them what the emergency is and what they are to do.
- Deaths in large scale fires attributed to 'panic' are far more likely to have been caused by delays in people receiving information about a fire.
- Fire alarm sirens cannot always be relied upon to prompt people to immediately move to safety.
- The start-up time (i.e. people's reaction to an alarm) is just as important as the time it takes to physically reach an exit.
- Much of the movement in the early stages of fires is characterised by investigation, not escape.
- As long as an exit is not seriously obstructed, people have a tendency to move in a familiar direction (the way they came in) even if further away, rather than to use a conventional unfamiliar fire escape route.
- Individuals often move towards and with group members and maintain proximity as far as possible with individuals to whom they have emotional ties.
- Fire exit signs are not always noticed (or recalled) and may not overcome difficulties in orientation and wayfinding imposed on escapees by the architectural layout and design of an escape route.
- People are often prepared, if necessary, to try to move through smoke.
- People's ability to move towards exits may vary considerably (for example, a young fit adult as opposed to a person who is elderly or who has a disability).[2]

# APPENDIX II: EXAMPLES OF SITE SAFETY SIGNS

No access for
unauthorised persons

Smoking and naked
flames forbidden

No smoking

Do not touch

No access for
pedestrians

Not drinkable

Do not extinguish
with water

No access for
industrial vehicles

Flammable material

Explosive material

Toxic material

Drop

Corrosive material

Biological risk

Overhead load

Obstacles

Industrial vehicles

Danger: electricity

General danger

Low temperature

Laser beam

Oxidant material

Non-ionising radiation

Radioactive material

Eye protection
must be worn

Safety helmet
must be worn

Ear protection
must be worn

Pedestrians must
use this route

Respiratory equipment
must be worn

Safety boots
must be worn

Safety gloves
must be worn

General mandatory sign
(to be accompanied
where necessary by
another sign)

Safety harness
must be worn

Face protection
must be worn

Safety overalls
must be worn

First-aid poster

Emergency telephone
for first aid or escape

Stretcher

Eyewash

Emergency exit escape route

Supplemtentary
directional escape
route

Emergency exit

167

# NOTES

## Chapter 1

1    There are two types of survey for asbestos: a management survey and a refurbishment/demolition survey. The purpose of a management survey is to manage asbestos during the normal occupation and use of a site and must identify any asbestos that could be damaged or disturbed by normal activities, including foreseeable maintenance. A refurbishment/demolition survey is required where the site – or part of it – needs refurbishment or demolition to ensure that such work is done by the right contractor in the right way and must locate and identify all asbestos before any work begins.

2    The Disclosure and Barring Service is a government agency that helps employers make safer recruitment decisions by processing and issuing DBS checks for England, Wales, the Channel Islands and the Isle of Man. DBS also maintains the adults' and children's Barred Lists and makes considered decisions as to whether an individual should be included on one or both of these lists and barred from engaging in regulated activity.

## Chapter 3

1    Health and Safety Executive, 'Why is asbestos dangerous?', *Health and Safety Executive* www.hse.gov.uk/asbestos/dangerous.htm (accessed 17 January 2020).

2    Health and Safety Executive, 'Construction statistics in Great Britain, 2019', *Health and Safety Executive – Annual Statistics*, www.hse.gov.uk/statistics/industry/construction.pdf, 2019 (accessed 25 February 2020).

3    Ibid.

4    Drones present a hazard to aviation and their use is regulated in law by the Air Navigation Order. More information is available on the government's website www.gov.uk/government/news/drones-are-you-flying-yours-safely-and-legally (accessed 26 January 2020).

5    The Confined Spaces Regulations 1997 impose legal duties on employers and self-employed people to ensure that work that needs to carried out in confined spaces is managed safely in accordance with the regulations.

6    Health and Safety Executive, 'Asthma', *Health and Safety Executive* www.hse.gov.uk/asthma (accessed 25 February 2020).

7    Health and Safety Executive, 'Silicosis', *Health and Safety Executive* www.hse.gov.uk/lung-disease/silicosis.htm (accessed 25 February 2020).

8   Health and Safety Executive, 'Chronic obstructive pulmonary disease (COPD)', *Health and Safety Executive* www.hse.gov.uk/copd/index.htm (accessed 25 February 2020).

9   The Control of Substances Hazardous to Health Regulations 2002 are intended to prevent or control exposure to substances that are hazardous to health and impose duties on employers to identify and control the use of such substances.

10  NHS, 'Leptospirosis (Weil's disease)', *NHS*, www.nhs.uk/conditions/ leptospirosis, 2020 (accessed 25 February 2020).

11  Health and Safety Executive, 'Harmful Micro-Organisms: Leptospirosis / Weil's Disease from rats', *Health and Safety Executive* www.hse.gov.uk/construction/ healthrisks/hazardous-substances/harmful-micro-organisms/leptospirosis-weils-disease.htm (accessed 25 February 2020).

12  RHS, 'Giant Hogweed', *RHS* www.rhs.org.uk/advice/profile?pid=458 (accessed 17 January 2020).

13  GOV.UK, 'Psittacosis', *GOV.UK* www.gov.uk/guidance/psittacosis, 2017 (accessed 17 January 2020).

14  Health and Safety Executive, 'Extrinsic Allergic Alveolitis', *Health and Safety Executive* www.hse.gov.uk/lung-disease/extrinsic-allergic-alveolitis.htm (accessed 17 January 2020).

15  NHS, 'Lyme disease', *NHS* www.nhs.uk/conditions/lyme-disease, 2018 (accessed 17 January 2020).

16  NHS, 'Insect Bites and Stings – Symptons', *NHS* www.nhs.uk/conditions/ insect-bites-and-stings/symptoms, 2019 (accessed 17 January 2020).

17  NHS, 'Snake bites', *NHS* www.nhs.uk/conditions/snake-bites, 2019 (accessed 17 January 2020).

Chapter 4

1   'Reasonably practicable' means balancing the level of risk against the measures needed to control the real risk in terms of money, time or trouble. You do not need to take action if it would be grossly disproportionate to the level of risk.

2   Cognitive diversity is defined as the differences in our thought and problem-solving processes. Our differences in terms of culture, background, experiences and personalities are core to diverse thought. Bringing together people who think differently from one another can create conversations that stimulate new ideas and innovation.

3   Health and Safety Executive, 'Fire safety in construction', *Health and Safety Executive* www.hse.gov.uk/pubns/books/hsg168.htm (accessed 17 January 2020).

4   Detailed guidance on the principles of fire safety are beyond the scope of this guidance.

5   Health and Safety Executive, 'Working at height', *Health and Safety Executive* www.hse.gov.uk/toolbox/height.htm (accessed 22 January 2020).

6   Health and Safety Executive, `Musculoskeletal disorders at work' https://www.hse.gov.uk/msd/index.htm (accessed 1 July 2020).

7   Health and Safety Executive, 'Construction dust', *Health and Safety Executive* www.hse.gov.uk/pubns/cis36.pdf (accessed 17 January 2020).

8   Health and Safety Executive, 'Assessing the slip resistance of flooring', *Health and Safety Executive* www.hse.gov.uk/pubns/geis2.pdf (accessed 22 January 2020).

9   Test data should be provided by an UKAS certified testing laboratory, or similar, and undertaken in accordance with the HSE's and UKSRG recommendations using a pendulum test in accordance with BS 7976.

10  Construction Industry Training Board, 'CDM2015 – Industry guidance for Designers', *Construction Industry Training Board 2015*, www.citb.co.uk/documents/cdm%20regs/2015/cdm-2015-designers-printer-friendly.pdf, 2015 (accessed 17 January 2020).

11  The Management of Health and Safety at Work Regulations 1999 s1 r4.

12  A safety management plan should include documented details of arrangements to implement, control, monitor and review measures required to manage the hazard identified that may pose a risk to employees.

## Chapter 5

1   The United Kingdom (UK) comprises England, Northern Ireland, Scotland and Wales. Although the UK is a unitary sovereign state, Northern Ireland, Scotland and Wales have an increasing degree of legislative autonomy through the process of devolution. Legislation enacted across Great Britain applies to England, Scotland and Wales.

2   The HSWA is applicable in England and Wales but all functions of the crown under the Act are devolved to the Welsh Assembly for projects undertaken in Wales.

3   The Building Act is applicable in England and Wales but all functions of the crown under the Act are devolved to the Welsh Assembly for projects undertaken in Wales.

4   Responsibility for Building Regulations in Wales is devolved to the Welsh Assembly.

5   As defined in Regulation 3 of The Regulatory Reform (Fire Safety) Order 2005.

6   England and Wales each have their own Approved Documents, tailored to suit the detail of the Building Regulations as they apply to each jurisdiction.

7   European Standards (ENs) are British Standards (BSs) that have been ratified by one of three European Standardisation Organisations. ENs will continue to be

applicable to projects undertaken in the UK following the UK's departure from the European Union.

8    Including products incorporated within building elements with the exception of power, control and communication cables which are covered by EN 13501-6

9    The fire performance of construction products may also be classified in the UK in accordance with BS 476 Fire tests on building materials and structures, which is referred to as the national classification. Table B1 of Approved Document B transposes the fire classifications from BS EN 13501-1 to the national classes set out in BS 476. The national classifications do not automatically equate with the transposed classifications in BS EN 13501-1 and therefore products cannot typically assume a European class unless they have been tested accordingly.

10   Health and Safety Executive, 'Legal Status of HSE guidance and ACOPs', *Health and Safety Executive* www.hse.gov.uk/legislation/legal-status.htm (accessed 29 January 2020).

11   'Reasonable steps' may require you to do more than is strictly required by law and regulations.

## Chapter 6

1    A domestic client is defined in the CDM Regulations as a client for whom a project is being carried out which is not in the course or furtherance of a business of that client.

2    The Construction Industry Training Board (CITB) has published guidance regarding all duties holders' responsibilities under the CDM Regulations that can be accessed on their website at CITB, 'Construction (Design and Management) Regulations', *CITB* www.citb.co.uk/about-citb/partnerships-and-initiatives/construction-design-and-management-cdm-regulations/cdm-regulations/ (accessed 22 January 2020).

3    Anyone that prepares, modifies, arranges for or instructs design work is deemed to be a designer under the CDM Regulations, including clients and contractors, and assumes the duties of a designer under the CDM Regulations. This includes anyone that may not be part of the project team but still instructs you in connection with your design. For example, if a planning officer instructs you to modify your design and that instruction does not directly relate to ensuring compliance with planning policy, that planning officer will be deemed to be a designer under the CDM Regulations.

4    For complex or unusual projects, it may be beneficial for the client to appoint a health and safety specialist to support the design team. Some clients also choose to appoint a health and safety or CDM adviser to advise them regarding their client duties, and may also choose to appoint the same specialist as the principal designer, but the duties of the two roles are distinct and should not be confused.

Chapter 7
1   Materials covered by the Classification Without Further Testing (CWFT) process can be found by accessing the European Commission's website eur-lex.europa. eu/
2   United Kingdom Accredited Service.
3   Details of best practice in conducting assessments and technical evaluations is provided in the Passive Fire Protection Forum's *Guide to undertaking technical assessments of the fire performance of construction products based on fire test evidence – 2019.*

Appendix
1   Canter, David V., *An Overview of Behaviour in Fires*, Psychology in Action. Dartmouth Benchmark Series, Dartmouth Publishing Company, Hampshire, UK (1996), pp. 159-188. http://eprints.hud.ac.uk/9228/1/CANTER_159.pdf.
2   Sime, Jonathan D., *Human Behaviour in Fires*, Building Use and Safety Research Unit, School of Architecture, Portsmouth Polytechnic, (1991).

# INDEX